The Middle Age of African History

EDITED BY

ROLAND OLIVER

LONDON
OXFORD UNIVERSITY PRESS
NAIROBI IBADAN
1967

Oxford University Press, Ely House, London W.1

GLASGOW NEW YORK TORONTO MELBOURNE WELLINGTON
CAPE TOWN SALISBURY IBADAN NAIROBI LUSAKA ADDIS ABABA
BOMBAY CALCUTTA MADRAS KARACHI LAHORE DACCA
KUALA LUMPUR HONG KONG TOKYO

Maps drawn by
REGMARAD

Printed in Great Britain by
Western Printing Services Ltd, Bristol

Foreword

LIKE ITS PREDECESSOR, *The Dawn of African History*, this volume presents a series of talks broadcast by the General Overseas Service of the B.B.C. *The Dawn of African History* was broadcast in 1958 and first published in 1961. *The Middle Age of African History* was broadcast between April and June 1967. Once again, the authors are all people who have made an original contribution to African history. Most of them represent a younger generation of scholars, trained since the earlier series was prepared. Their work is new work, dealing with peoples and topics not mentioned in the earlier series. Though still concerned entirely with pre-colonial Africa, most of the essays deal with a period somewhat later in time than those included in *The Dawn of African History*. Partly for this reason, and partly because of the progress of knowledge during the past ten years, *The Middle Age of African History* seems an appropriate title.

The contributors wish to record their gratitude to Miss Dorothy Grenfell-Williams of the B.B.C.

Contents

v

List of Maps

CHAPTER ONE

Medieval Nubia

P. L. Shinnie

IN THE YEAR 639 the Arabs swept into Egypt and made conquests throughout North Africa. But there was just one region where they did not have an immediate success. The land which resisted this first tide of Arab conquests was Nubia, which lies along the Nile to the south of Egypt. The Arabs met redoubtable opponents when they tried to advance south into Nubia, which had been a Christian state for a hundred years. And indeed Nubia continued to form a barrier to Arab and Muslim expansion for nearly eight hundred years. The existence of this Christian power strongly influenced the political development of north-east Africa. It meant that while Islam was spreading throughout the north and much of the west of Africa, its advance into what is now the Sudan was long delayed, with important results for that country. It was only after the final collapse of the Christian kingdom of Dongola in the fourteenth century that Islam finally triumphed.

It is perhaps surprising to find that far up the Nile there were Christian kings and Christian states which lasted for over eight hundred years. These states had an organization and a rich culture, deeply influenced by Byzantine Greece. Yet the people of Nubia, living in a barren and poor land, squeezed by the desert on either side into a narrow strip along the river, developed their own distinctive civilization. They wrote in their own language, as well as in Greek and Coptic. They built churches and monasteries and towns. Certainly their culture owed a lot to outside influences, but

1

equally certainly it evolved into something distinctively Nubian.

Until recently very little was known of these people, whose descendants still live in the area today and still speak the same Nubian language. But in the last few years there have been many archaeological expeditions to the area which is being flooded as a result of the building of the Aswan high dam. This means that we now have a far more detailed picture of the life and culture of the medieval Nubians than was possible before. We can fill in the details of art and daily life which were lacking in the sparse historical records given to us by the Arab writers, who were previously the main source of information.

The outline of Nubian history is reasonably clear. It looks as if people of Nubian speech moved into the Nile Valley from the west during the first few centuries A.D. They formed a number of pagan principalities along the Nile stretching far south from Aswan. In the middle of the sixth century Christian missionaries arrived, travelling upstream from Egypt. The missionaries were rapidly successful. By the end of the century, at least the rulers of the country as far south as modern Khartoum had adopted Christianity as their religion. Today we have tangible evidence of the success of the new religion. For throughout the area there are many ruined churches, which we know to have been built from about the middle of the seventh century onwards. And it is not only the churches which show the hold of Christianity on Nubia. The surviving examples of Nubian secular art, particularly the beautiful and elaborately patterned pottery, are often decorated with Christian symbols and designs.

Three Nubian kingdoms developed along the River Nile: Nobatia in the north, Makuria centred on Old Dongola farther south, and Alwa farther south again in the region of the junction of the Blue and White Niles. We have the names of many rulers and information on their relations with Islamic Egypt, which were sometimes friendly and sometimes hostile.

We know that Nubia was at the height of its political and military power during the ninth and tenth centuries, the period when Egypt was ruled by the Fatimid dynasty.

Friendly relations developed between the Christian Nubians and the Islamic Fatimids. This was partly because of the military strength of the Nubians. The Fatimids felt it wise to be friendly with such a well-armed neighbour. But it was also partly because the Nubians had given the Fatimids active help during their struggle for power in Egypt. Certainly the Nubians were regarded as an important power throughout the Muslim world. As evidence of this we can cite the deep impression made by the middle of the ninth century by a Nubian embassy at Baghdad, the capital of the Abbasid Caliphs.

I have said that the ninth and tenth centuries saw the height of Nubia's political and military power. This was also the time of its greatest cultural development. The archaeological work of the last five years has shown us that Nubia was by no means a cultural backwater. On the contrary it was a country of very considerable artistic achievement. The richness of this achievement can be seen in the pottery and in the paintings which adorned the churches. The pottery has been known for many years, but it is only recently, by the careful excavation of many sites, that it has been possible to put the different types into order of date. Now that this has been done we can see that the very beautiful and characteristic painted pottery was made during the period from about A.D. 800–1000 which is, in fact, the peak period of Nubian civilization.

This pottery, finely made and elaborately painted, is a very remarkable product and, except for the glazed Islamic wares of Near Eastern inspiration made in Egypt, it is the most beautiful pottery ever produced in Africa. There are certainly traces of outside cultural influences on the designs of this beautiful ware. There are themes which suggest the pottery of the earlier Meroitic state, and animal designs which owe something to Fatimid Egypt and Sassanian Persia. But in spite of these hints of other cultures Nubian ceramic art is distinctive and unique.

The recent study of the pottery also tells us something of trade conditions and the ebb and flow of contact with Egypt. In the early part of this period there is evidence that some pottery was imported from Egypt, particularly the large two-handled jars used for transporting wine. After about A.D. 750–800 this flow of pottery into Nubia from Egypt seems to have come to an end. And it was round about that time that the magnificent local pot-making seems to have started. Pottery imports on a large scale did not start again until after about A.D. 1000.

The other startling discovery of the last few years has been the quality of the paintings which decorated the churches. A recent Polish expedition discovered a cathedral at Faras, north of Dongola. The cathedral was intact except for its roof, as it had been protected by a sand-dune which had collected over it. This is probably the most important ecclesiastical building in the whole of Nubia and it was richly decorated with paintings on all its inside walls. In many cases later paintings had been superimposed on earlier ones, so that it is now possible to get an idea of changes in style and thus to begin to make a chronology of Nubian painting. The surprising thing about these paintings is how closely they conform to Byzantine styles and how little they seem to owe to the traditions of the Copts—the Christian community in Egypt. The inscriptions which accompany them are sometimes in Coptic and sometimes in Greek, whilst a few are in the old Nubian language of the country and a few scribbles are in Arabic.

There is more evidence of the power of the Byzantine influence to be found on gravestones dating from as late as the twelfth century. They are engraved with prayers of the Orthodox Church, written in Greek. This is remarkable, because direct contact with the Byzantine world must have been very difficult for the Nubians after the Arab conquest of Egypt in A.D. 639.

The Faras paintings include a magnificent nativity scene as well as pictures of saints, bishops and royalty—there is a particularly interesting picture of a queen mother. They provide rich material for the study of the artistic development and cultural history of Nubia and, as I have said, they have also made it possible for us to give much more precise dates to different artistic styles. Another striking discovery in the cathedral was that of a list written on the wall of a side chapel, giving the names and lengths of reigns of a long series of bishops. The list does not give dates, but precisely dated gravestones of some of these bishops have been found, and so it is now possible to establish both the names and dates of the Bishops of Faras, perhaps the senior see of the Nubian Church.

Recent work has given us many other fascinating details. For instance, in my own excavations of a large ruined town at Debeira, carried out for the University of Ghana, we found for the first time a complete town layout, and we can see what the ordinary houses of the medieval Nubians were like. These houses were built of sun-dried brick. They consisted of three or more rooms and they were roofed with an ingenious type of vault, not known elsewhere. We also found examples of the special dishes used for baking bread, stones for grinding grain and other domestic objects which enable us to build up a picture of daily life.

On the historical side, probably the most dramatic discoveries have been at Qasr Ibrim, a little farther north. Here archaeologists found a cache of documents in old Nubian, which doubled the amount of written material known to us in that language. The grave of a bishop was discovered too. He was still wearing his ecclesiastical robes, and buried with him were two documents giving details of his consecration as bishop in the year 1373—many years after it had been thought that Christianity had vanished from the region. So our ideas of the religious, and also perhaps the political, history of the region need to be revised. It now appears that the Arab incursions of the fourteenth century may have taken longer to establish Islam in Nubia than has usually been thought.

Another interesting new aspect is the evidence that is now accumulating that Arabs were living in parts of Nubia from the tenth century onwards. This evidence is to be found in a number of gravestones of Muslims, written in Arabic, which have recently been found, some of them in cemeteries which are predominantly Christian. These indicate the presence of a Muslim population and suggest that the two communities were living together in amity for some centuries. Indeed the existence of that bishop at Qasr Ibrim late in the fourteenth century may turn out to be further evidence that, whoever had the political power, toleration was practised by both religions.

Looking then at what we now know of Nubian history we can see that it was an important participant in the history of north-east Africa during the medieval period. And Nubia's was not merely a passive influence. On occasions at least, the kings of Nubia acted as the protectors of the Coptic Christians of Egypt. Nubian armies occupied parts of upper Egypt at various times during the ninth and tenth centuries, and on one occasion even reached Cairo.

Finally the very existence of the Christian lands of Nubia had one other important influence on the course of African history. The Nubian lands lay right across the natural east–west trade route south of the Sahara. This meant that, at least until the end of the fourteenth century and probably later, West African traders from the Muslim states along the River Niger had to pass northwards across the desert rather than east through Christian Nubia. The northern route led the West African traders and travellers through centres of Islamic influence and finally to Cairo. And thus they were kept in closer contact with the mainstream of Islamic culture than they would have been if the way which lies south of the desert had been open to them.

CHAPTER TWO

Christian Ethiopia

E. Haberland

ETHIOPIA belongs neither to the Islamic culture of North Africa nor to the Negro culture of sub-Saharan Africa. To discover the influences on the development of this highland region we have to look elsewhere, to the ancient culture of South Arabia, and to Christianity, which took root in Ethiopia in the fourth century.

In the centuries immediately before and after the birth of Christ the classical world was dominated by the ideas of Greece and Rome. During this period there was a great expansion in the trade between Europe and the Near East and India. The South Arabians were well placed to take advantage of this trade. At this time they dominated the Red Sea and they established many trading centres along its shores. The expansion of trade brought new prosperity to the South Arabians and their culture blossomed.

Along the western shores of the Red Sea the South Arabians not only set up trading posts on the coast of Eritrea, they also invaded the Ethiopian highlands farther inland. There they assimilated the native Cushitic population. Over the centuries various small states came into being. The best known of these was Aksum and in the course of numerous wars the kings of Aksum were able to unify the various Semitic-speaking groups of northern Ethiopia and also to subjugate the restless nomads, who were harassing the caravan routes to the Nile. Aksum, from the second century to the fifth century A.D., was the most important state in the Red Sea area. Close links developed between Aksum and the great Christian Byzantine Empire which had evolved from the Roman Empire. This relationship grew closer still with the introduction of Christianity in Aksum in the fourth century. Christianity soon became the state religion there.

But the greatness of Aksum came to an end with the great tide of Arab conquests in the seventh century. It was cut off by the Arabs from its Christian allies to the north, and it was deprived of its economic foundation by the diversion of the great trade routes. Aksum was reduced to trying to survive. Finally it vanished entirely. Ethiopia was completely passed over in the dark ages of history from about A.D. 600 to 1100. Much of what had been introduced to Ethiopia by the South Arabians and their friends vanished; but what did remain was important. In spite of the cultural decline, Christianity was firmly rooted. It spread with the expansion of the Semitic-speaking peoples in Ethiopia. The art of writing, although it was limited to the clergy, resulted in the development of a literature, of chronicles and of a genuine awareness of history. What actually happened in those centuries cannot at present be reconstructed. It is sufficient to know that Aksum lost its importance as a capital, although right up to the nineteenth century some Ethiopian kings were enthroned within its walls. The centre of gravity of Christian Ethiopia moved farther and farther south. In 1268 there emerges the figure of King Yekuna Amlak, who claimed to be the legitimate descendant of the ancient dynasty of Aksum, henceforward known as the 'Solomonic dynasty'.

With this official restoration of the Aksumite kingdom, from now on usually called Ethiopia, an entirely new chapter of history begins. It was no longer an empire which drew its main inspiration from the Roman Mediterranean. The model and ideal of the Ethiopian empire were from now on based on the holy books of Christianity, the Old and New Testaments of the Bible, and above all on the history of the great kings of Israel. Of supreme importance was a literary work, probably compiled by an Ethiopian monk, which became famous under the title of *Kebra Nagast*, which means 'The Glory of the Kings'. The *Kebra Nagast* is a collection of ancient oriental legends from the Old Testament, the Talmud, the Koran, and from Eastern Christian, Jewish and Islamic folklore. These were collected together and tailored to suit the kingdom of Ethiopia and its dynasty. This work, and its importance for the historical task of Ethiopia, can only be compared to the importance of Vergil's *Aeneid* to the Roman Empire.

The most important part of the *Kebra Nagast* has its origins in the Old Testament. In the Old Testament there is a brief mention of the visit of the Queen of Sheba to King Solomon in Jerusalem. In the *Kebra Nagast* the Queen of Sheba becomes the Queen of Ethiopia who, in the course of her visit, meets King Solomon and bears him a son. This son, called Menelik, becomes the first King of Ethiopia and founder of the legal dynasty ruling Ethiopia to this day. It is called the 'Solomonic dynasty' after its great ancestor. The *Kebra Nagast* goes on to relate that Menelik grew up at his mother's home. While he was still a young man he visited his father in Jerusalem. Solomon welcomed him with great joy and gave him, as an escort, the firstborn sons of the noble families of the twelve tribes of Israel, in order that Israel should also rule in Ethiopia. Before they left Jerusalem the young men secretly removed from the Temple the Ark of the Covenant and brought it to Aksum. And so the Holy of Holies of Israel came to Ethiopia.

Thus the *Kebra Nagast* explains that the kings of Ethiopia are the descendants of the Israelite kings of the Old Testament, and representatives of the Old Covenant which God concluded with David. And so, the argument goes, the Ethiopians are also the new Chosen People of God because they have, unlike the Jews, acknowledged Jesus Christ as the Redeemer. Further, the Ethiopian kings are also physically related to Jesus Christ, for they share with him the same ancestors. This divine mandate, suggested by the *Kebra Nagast*, determined the future development of Ethiopia into a Holy Empire. And the conviction it gave the Ethiopians helped them to become the creative power in the sphere over which they were to rule. A title, used earlier by the kings of Aksum, was revived about this time. The rulers of Christian Ethiopia call themselves the 'King of Kings of Ethiopia' —usually translated into English as Emperor—in order to express their sovereignty over any other rulers within their sphere of influence. This faith in a divine mission was to have a powerful effect on the future of the Ethiopian dynasty. It is difficult to explain how, without it, the small state of the Amhara could ever have been able to undertake the vast labour of colonizing the southern parts of Ethiopia.

Indeed it is astonishing to see what these dynamic people were able to achieve, spurred on by their sense of mission. In the fourteenth and fifteenth centuries large areas of northern Ethiopia were still inhabited by other tribes. These were added to the Ethiopian empire by military aggression, but also by intense peaceful assimilation and missionary work. The chronicles of the medieval kings tend to concentrate on the military achievements of the rulers. So it is only too easy to overlook the work of the missionary monks who have entered into Ethiopian church history as saints. Upholding the cross, they entered territories where no Ethiopian armies had set foot before. They subjugated pagan kings and peoples by the power of their teaching, and as the chronicles say they 'enlightened Ethiopia by their faith'. At this time, many peoples of the Ethiopian south, who later fell back into heathendom, were converted to Christianity and were connected with the empire as tributary states. Examples were the country of Enarya, with its wealth of gold, and the powerful Kaffa, with its coffee forests, and the unassailable Janjero.

However, it was not only missionary monks who advanced towards the south, but also kings, army commanders, governors and princes. The kings sought to spread the gospel and to expand the political influence of Ethiopia; the rest hoped to gain riches and to achieve new honours. As an example of these southern conquests, we may take the kingdom of Wolamo. According to tradition, the kingdom was conquered by Michael, a nobleman from the north who travelled to Wolamo with a small entourage of priests, pages and mounted knights. The invaders had courage and superior weapons. Their mounted knights were terrifying, since horse-riding had been unknown to the southerners until then. In spite of these advantages, they were on the verge of losing the battle owing to their small number. The tide turned when they employed the stratagem of throwing towards the attacking Wolamo, not their spears but woven dresses and beautiful jewellery, precious foreign rarities to the Wolamo. The Wolamo were amazed and came to the conclusion that anyone who was so rich and mighty was entitled to seize the authority in their country. Thus, a Christian dynasty came to power. Certainly the story illustrates the greater sophistication of the Christian Ethiopians. And indeed it was not only their religion which the Christian invaders brought to the south. They brought a sophisticated culture which had a profound influence on the old south Ethiopian patterns of life. They introduced, for instance, the craft of weaving, the crafts of working gold and silver, improvements in house-building, and many new cultivable plants. In the many small kingdoms of the south, there developed an almost-modern administration, with a well-run fiscal and judicial system, with carefully maintained stone walls and wide, well-kept roads. The Court ceremonial was enlarged by many new offices, and state councils were set up nearly everywhere. With the introduction of horse and mule, a nearly feudal knighthood developed, whose members were invested by the kings with land and honours, and who held the most important offices of state.

We ought not to forget, however, that all this was over-shadowed by the sense of mission of the Ethiopian rulers, who not only won new provinces and tributaries for their empire, but also, faithful to the promises of the *Kebra Nagast*, spread the Christian Holy Order in the part of the world appointed to them. They held to their mission even in times of great political stress. For instance, in 1595 the Jewish mountain dwellers in the heart of the empire rose in rebellion, the Turks threatened the north, and the wild hordes of the warlike Galla people invaded the empire from the east. Nevertheless in that year King Sarsa Dengel undertook an expedition to the south Ethiopian kingdom of Enarya, at the invitation of its ruler, in order to introduce Christianity there and to christen the king.

From the end of the seventeenth century, the Ethiopian empire gradually declined, as a result of internal unrest, weak rulers and, above all, the invasion of the Galla and the subsequent devastation of the country. The Galla permanently occupied many up to then Christian regions, and broke the connexion between the north and the south. Without any contact with the Christian empire in the north, the converted peoples of the south sank back into heathendom, although the glorious times of the conversion to Christianity were always remembered. Kings and noblemen of many southern states proudly recalled the origin of their descendants from the north.

In spite of this interruption of several centuries, the profound influence of the culture of the north is still obvious today. When, towards the end of the last century, with the second restoration of the Solomonic dynasty, the empire expanded once more, this meant not only the reunification of the provinces of Christian Ethiopia in the north, but also the reconquest of the lost provinces in the south, where the empire had formerly exercised its divine mission.

CHAPTER THREE

The Long March of Islam in the Western Sudan

Nehemiah Levtzion

THE EXPANSION OF ISLAM into tropical Africa began well over a thousand years ago. In the centuries since then two parallel processes have been at work. On the one hand vast areas of Africa have been Islamized. On the other hand Islam has been Africanized. Indeed throughout the world Islam has shown itself to be a faith which can pass readily from one civilization to another. Islam has spread among Hindus and Buddhists, among the peoples of central Asia and south-eastern Europe. This success is only partly to be explained by military conquest. In Africa, traders rather than warriors have been its principal agents.

The Sahara, one of the world's most inhospitable, arid zones, cut tropical Africa off from the northern shores of the continent, which are part of the Mediterranean and Muslim civilizations. But the Sahara was by no means an absolute barrier. Nomadic tribes, in origin branches of the Berber confederations of North Africa, crossed the Sahara and in-habited the oases and the southern fringes of the desert. They controlled the trans-Saharan trails, over which the salt of the Sahara was carried to be traded for the gold of the Sudan, 'the country of the black people'. Following the Arab con-quest of North Africa in the seventh century, Islam spread among the Berbers, and the rich gold trade became the monopoly of the Muslims. Through these traders the name

Ghana, 'the country of the gold', became known in the Muslim world. It was first mentioned by an Arab geographer of the eighth century.

Lying far to the north of present-day Ghana, this ancient kingdom was the most powerful of several kingdoms which rose in the Sahel, 'the shore' of the desert sea of the Sahara. Located in this strategic zone, Ghana controlled the gold trade and attracted the Muslim traders. In the middle of the eleventh century there was a Muslim town right next to the royal capital of Ghana. Muslims, distinguished by their literacy, served as ministers and interpreters to the king of Ghana. The King himself still followed his ancestral religion, although two of his neighbours, the king of Takrur on the River Senegal to the west, and the king of Gao on the Niger River to the east, had both become followers of Islam under the influence of Muslim traders. In 1076 things were to change in Ghana too. In that year Ghana was conquered by the Almoravids. The Almoravids were a group of militant Muslims who arose among the Berbers of the south-western Sahara. In fact they only ruled over Ghana for eleven years. But they had an important influence, because they stimulated the spread of Islam by destroying the citadel of the pagan king of Ghana. In the century that followed, the twelfth century, we find that Ghana is described as a Muslim kingdom. But it was only a shadow of its past. By then new forces had emerged. The most important of these was Mali. And Mali became the dominant force in the western Sudan during the thirteenth and fourteenth centuries.

The political power shifted from Ghana, right at the gates of the Sahara, southwards to Mali on the upper Niger. This change was probably associated with the extension of the trade routes southwards in search of new and richer sources of gold. The enterprising traders who opened up the new routes between the termini of the trans-Saharan trails and the sources of the gold were Sudanese, that is black Africans. Naturally, in the course of their business, these black African traders came into close contact with the Muslims of North Africa. Through their trade they became detached from the agricultural and tribal ways of life, in which the traditional African religions are anchored. They adopted Islam more easily and in their wanderings could find hospitality as well as a sense of community among Muslims in the new trading centres which developed along the trade routes. Thus, Berber traders brought Islam down to the fringes of tropical Africa and Sudanese traders took over and carried it much farther to the south.

Muslims were engaged in the trade, but it was the traditional African chiefs who controlled it, drawing income and power out of it. Thus traders were in close communication with chiefs. Chiefs used Muslims as scribes, commissioned them as ambassadors and collected from them information about neighbouring countries, for the network of Muslim communities became a most effective network of communications. Employing Muslims in their courts, the chiefs could not escape their religious influence.

Indeed the chiefs were particularly open to influence, because the development of new states out of the old kinship units was putting new and complicated strains on them. Farther to the south, where the moulding of the new political institutions was sheltered from the direct influence of Islam, the ancestral religion was able to develop and fuse with the more elaborate political system. But where the political development almost coincided with the coming of Islam, chiefs tended to seek spiritual support from the Muslims. The Muslims had impressive prayers and carried charms containing Koranic verses. Al-Bakri, an eleventh-century geographer, describes the conversion of the chief of a Mande principality by a Muslim who saved the country from drought after all the efforts of the local priests had failed. Only the chief and his lieutenants became Muslims, while the ordinary people remained pagans. Many traditional stories have similar themes. Chiefs did not become Muslims overnight, nor did they renounce the old religion at once. Rather they set out on a cultural and religious path leading towards Islam. Some stopped along the way, adopting a middle position between Islam and paganism. Others came nearer to being complete Muslims. This was the case of the royal house of Mali in its prime.

From their centre on the upper Niger, south of Bamako, where they had been reached by the influence of the African Muslim traders, the kings of Mali extended their empire northwards in the thirteenth century. And they captured the former territories of Ghana, where the Muslim element became more and more important. Here they came into direct contact with the Muslim world through the trans-Saharan trade. Their adherence to Islam grew stronger as the new religion gave them access to the wider world. They entered into diplomatic relations with the Sultans of Morocco and some of them went on pilgrimages to Mecca, visiting Cairo on the way. Islamic ceremonies attended by the king are described by Ibn-Battuta, the Moroccan traveller who visited Mali in 1352–3. But he points also to strong survivals of the old religion and its customs.

In the fifteenth century the pattern of power was changing again in the western Sudan. The vast empire of Mali disintegrated and the kingdom of Songhai expanded in its place. The hero of Songhai's rise to power and influence was Sonni Ali, who continued a line of chiefs whose Islamic faith was rather weak. He himself dared to persecute the Muslim scholars of Timbuktu for their link with his adversaries, the nomad Tuareg. When Sonni Ali died in 1493, one of the army commanders deposed his son and founded a new dynasty. Because he had overthrown the legitimate dynasty the new ruler, Askiya Muhammad, could not rely on the support accorded to the political system by the traditional religion. Being a Muslim himself, he set about making the Islamic faith a state religion. He went on a pilgrimage to Mecca, supported Muslim scholars and consulted them on state affairs.

His dynasty ruled over Songhai for about a century until its destruction by a Moroccan expeditionary force in 1591.

The Moroccan conquest caused a disruption of the political system of the great empires of the western Sudan. In the seventeenth and eighteenth centuries there were no great states with Muslim rulers in this area. This was a period of decline for Islam in the political sphere, with the passing away of its great patrons. But it was not, as some would argue, a period of stagnation. It was during this period that Muslim traders carried Islam still farther south, and brought the chiefs in the woodland savannah under the influence of Islam. Distinguished by their long robes, Muslims have always been a minority in this region, representing a new culture. But they have been integrated into the social and political system, and they have infused Islamic elements into the culture of the local states. This, for example, was the pattern in the north of modern Ghana. The contribution of chiefs to the spread of Islam is well marked by the fact that Islam has hardly gained any ground among the loosely organized societies, those known as 'tribes without rulers'.

From the fifteenth to the seventeenth centuries the celebrated Songhai town of Timbuktu had its golden age as the main collecting point of the trans-Saharan trade and as a centre of Islamic learning which rivalled famous centres in North Africa. In its mosques and schools eminent scholars taught religious and literary subjects. It resembled a university campus, as students studied particular subjects with masters who became specialized in different branches of Islamic learning. Timbuktu attracted Moorish and Berber scholars from the Saharan tribes. These white Muslims were predominant among the scholars of Timbuktu and they maintained close relations with the Muslim world across the Sahara. But their orientation to the north was matched by their loyalty to the Askiya of Songhai. This loyalty brought them into conflict with the Moroccan invaders when these arrived. Timbuktu was linked by the Niger waterway to

Jenne, over two hundred miles up the river. Jenne was another cultural centre, but unlike Timbuktu the scholars of Jenne were Sudanese, that is black Africans. From Jenne a network of trade routes extended southwards. And through the trade routes the cultural influence of the black African Muslims spread too.

Timbuktu and Jenne constituted the fountains which fed the streams of Islam flowing to the south. They supported the influence of the small and remote Muslim communities which carried the burden of the spread of Islam. These pioneers of Islam showed a certain degree of compromise in presenting Islam to the chiefs and the local population. It was the strength of Islam that it did not try to break through in its full vigour but made its impact in a mild form. It may seem surprising that Muslims in the outposts of Islam, living for many generations among unbelievers, still managed to preserve their Islamic standards. There are traditional stories of a few isolated Muslims who turned pagan, but on the whole they stayed firm in their faith. This was because of the continuous communication with stronger Muslim centres, the pilgrimages performed by quite a few individuals and the existence of the written code of Islam, the Koran and the books of Islamic law. Learning was the vital core of Islam and it has never been abandoned.

Through the living scholarly tradition and the links with the outside Muslim world, Islam in West Africa had a period of new vigour in the nineteenth century, when a series of religious wars engulfed the whole width of the northern belt of the Sudan, from the Atlantic coast to the Nile. The military success of Muslim movements in these wars brought Muslim scholars, men of religion, to political power. Under their rule Islam became not only another cultural feature of the state but the very reason of its existence. This gave new impetus to the spread of Islam and strengthened its hold over peoples long under Muslim influence. It was at that stage in the long march of Islam that Africa was conquered by the colonial powers.

CHAPTER FOUR

The Rise of the Akan

Adu Boahen

ACCORDING TO THE 1960 CENSUS OF GHANA, the Akan constitute 44·7 per cent of the entire population of the modern state. They include the Asante (Ashanti), the Akyem, the Kwahu, the Fante, the Wassa, the Assin and the Akuapem. All these people speak the same language, namely Twi or Akan. And they also share identical social and political institutions. For instance they all follow the Forty Day Calendar; they all have the same marriage and naming rites; they all have a matrilineal system of inheritance, that is one based on the idea that it is through the mother that the birthright of each family passes from generation to generation; and they all share a traditional law which rules that it is forbidden to choose a marriage partner from within your maternal or your paternal clan. Very closely related to the Akan, ethnically, culturally and linguistically, are the Guan, the Bono, the Sefwi and the Nzima of Ghana and the Baule and the Anyi of Ivory Coast.

Our knowledge of the history of this dominant section of the population of Ghana has greatly increased over the last ten years. Until about ten years ago we had to rely mainly on oral traditions and the published sources in English which were used by earlier historians such as Ward and Claridge. But recently new work on published and unpublished sources in Portuguese, Danish, Dutch and Arabic has added considerably to our store of knowledge of Akan history. We have also been helped by new archaeological discoveries and detailed study of the Akan language.

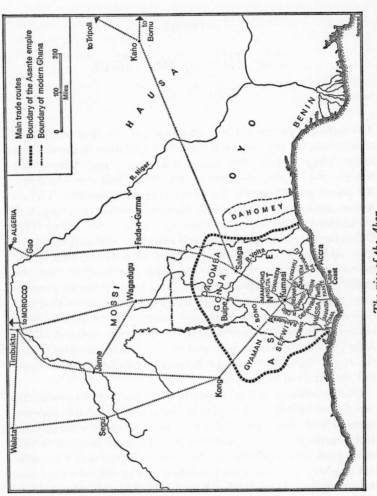

The rise of the Akan

Many historians were once of the opinion that these Akan peoples, as well as the two other principal peoples of southern Ghana, the Ewe and the Ga-Adangbe, migrated from the east and north into Ghana only in the fifteenth and sixteenth centuries. It now appears from linguistic and archaeological evidence that all these peoples have been living in Ghana for well over a thousand years, and that it was in Ghana that their languages and cultural and social institutions finally crystallized.

The evolution of the Akan cluster of peoples probably occurred in the area round the confluence of the Pra and Ofin rivers, just south of modern Kumasi. This area was and still is very rich in gold and kola nuts. Both these commodities were in great demand in the western Sudan and northern Africa, and by the thirteenth century commercial relations were established by the Akan with the Mande peoples of the upper Niger and with the Hausa people to the north of the lower Niger. Through the Mande and the Hausa, the Akan participated in the trans-Saharan trade with North Africa, Europe and the Middle East. The Akan also traded with the Guan and Ga peoples to the south of them, principally in cloth and beads imported from Benin, but also in salt and fish. The Akan increased in wealth, mainly as a result of these early commercial activities before the arrival of the Europeans. They therefore began to disperse northwards and southwards in clan or lineage groups to carve out kingdoms for themselves. These groups of Akan are known today by the kingdoms they formed. For example the Asante are those Akan who moved north and founded the Asante state, which as we shall see they transformed into an empire, and the Akyem are those who moved eastwards across the Pra River.

All the kingdoms and empires founded by the Akan had the monarchical system of government. The kings and queens were, and still are, elected from a single royal family, usually the founding family, which belongs to one of the eight matrilineal clans into which all the Akan are divided.

It is clear from Portuguese records that when they arrived on the coast of Ghana in the 1470s a number of states were already in existence, not only along the coast but also in the interior. The arrival of the Europeans and the opening up of the Atlantic added a new dimension to the commerce of the Akan. A steady increase in population and wealth followed, and this led to a rapid multiplication of their states. There is a most revealing map of what is now southern Ghana as it was in 1629, on which a great number of states are shown. Thirty-four of these states are named and twenty-eight of them are Akan.

It is clear from oral traditions, as well from the records of the Dutch, Danish and English trading companies, that the seventeenth century saw a bitter competition among the Akan states both for political supremacy and for the domination of the trade routes, especially to the coast. Some states were able to grow at the expense of others. During the next one hundred years one state after another was to emerge supreme in the western region. First Twifo, then Adansi, then Assin and finally Denkyira. In the eastern region Akyem and Akwamu, founded by clan groups which emigrated from the states of Adansi and Twifo across the Pra, gained an early lead over the Guan and Akan states by the beginning of the seventeenth century. By the turn of that century Akwamu had established her sway not only over Akyem and Kwahu but also over the coastal kingdoms of Accra and even across the Volta, over the Ewe states. A map of Ghana drawn in 1750 shows that by that date all these competing states had been absorbed by two main ones; the sprawling empire of Asante and the relatively much smaller kingdom of Fante extending about one hundred and fifty miles along the coast and twenty miles inland.

The Asante empire was the product of an intelligent blend of shrewd diplomacy and naked force. The nucleus of the empire was five kingdoms founded within a radius of some thirty miles from Kumasi by families who all belonged to the same line of the Oyoko matrilineal clan. Probably these Oyoko clan groups entered the area during the second half of the seventeenth century. They came from the region around the confluence of the Ofin and the Pra. The five kingdoms which formed the basis of the Asante empire were Kumasi, Dwaben, Bekwai, Kokofu and Nsuta. To this day the kings of the first four of these regard themselves as 'brothers' and they look on the king of the fifth as their 'uncle'. So, instead of competing among themselves as earlier Akan states had done, they co-operated together very closely. The leader of this group of Oyoko states was Osei Tutu, the king of Kumasi, who is referred to in the early eighteenth-century European records as 'the great Asante Caboceer Zaay'. In an attempt to increase the area of influence of the Oyoko states this king of Kumasi attempted to bring in the neighbouring non-Oyoko states. His attempt was made much easier by the common hatred of all these states for Denkyira. Oral traditions are unanimous on the oppressive nature of the Denkyira yoke and this is corroborated from documentary sources. For instance, Bosman, a contemporary Dutch observer of the 1680s, describes Denkyira as 'elevated by its great riches and power', and 'so arrogant that it looked on all negroes with a contemptible eye, esteeming them no more than slaves'.

So that he might endow his new union of states with a soul and a sacred and everlasting symbol of power, unity and stability, the king of Kumasi, Osei Tutu, and his 'chief priest' created the Golden Stool. Or, as oral traditions persistently and vociferously maintain, he brought the Golden Stool down from the sky. This stool soon became the rallying point of the Asante and even today is regarded by them with the utmost veneration. Osei Tutu went on to devise a constitution, a national army organized into four wings, a supreme court of appeal and the national Odwira or harvest festival. These nation-building devices of Osei Tutu proved so effective that members of the Union soon developed a sense of identity and national consciousness which grew in intensity with the years.

Having constructed this hard and sacred core of an empire Osei Tutu and his successor Opoku Ware, who ruled from 1720 until 1750, together with their confederate kings, embarked on a course of conquest. Their main aim was to gain control of the trade routes radiating northwards and southwards from the region of Kumasi, and to defeat the domineering people of Denkyira. They conquered Denkyira and her tributary states of Wassa, Sefwi, Aowin, Assin and Twifo between 1699 and 1701; between 1722 and 1745 Takyiman, Gyaman, Gonja and Dagomba to the north and north-west were vanquished; and between 1742 and 1744 so were Akyem, Accra and Akwamu to the south-east. In other words, by 1750 virtually all the Akan states of modern Ghana and Gyaman in the Ivory Coast had been incorporated into the Asante empire.

The only kingdom in southern Ghana which was able to resist the Asante imperial drive was the old kingdom of Fante. Indeed the Fante reacted to Asante expansionism by streamlining their political organization. And at the beginning of the eighteenth century they conquered and annexed the ancient coastal principalities of Kommenda, Asebu and Fetu to the west of them and Agona to the east.

So by the middle of the eighteenth century the area of modern Ghana, and parts of Ivory Coast and Togo, had been partitioned among these two Akan people, the Asante and the Fante, with the lion's share going to the Asante, thanks to the nationalist spirit, martial ardour and political genius of their leaders. As the Fante persistently refused to allow the Asante direct access to European forts on the coast, relations between the two powers remained strained throughout the eighteenth century and it was mainly the energetic support of the British which enabled them to maintain their independence. However during the first two decades of the nineteenth century, by exploiting the weakness of the British on the coast, the Asante finally accomplished the reduction and annexation of the Fante kingdom; thereby they achieved the first political unification of the states and peoples of modern Ghana, Ivory Coast and Togo.

How did the Asante govern their huge empire? It used to be generally accepted that, in the words of the historian Claridge, 'though the Ashantees could conquer, they could not govern, in fact they never made any serious attempt to do so'. It is now clear from the records of the eighteenth and nineteenth centuries that this view is wholly erroneous. As Bowdich learnt in Kumasi in 1816, Osei Tutu and Opoku Ware placed each subject ruler 'under the immediate care of some Ashantee chief, generally resident in the capital', and imposed on him an annual tribute. However, since these chiefs hardly ever visited their client states, this system of administration proved ineffective. Later rulers, particularly Osei Kwadwo, who reigned from 1765 to 1777, and Osei Bonsu, whose dates were 1801 to 1824, therefore revolutionized the old system. Cruickshank has described these changes most graphically: 'The King was not content to leave the government entirely in the hands of the native chiefs, who might possibly, in the course of time, rally the prostrate energies of the country, and combine to throw off his yoke. In consequence of this suspicion . . . he appointed pro-consuls of the Ashantee race, men of trust and confidence, to reside with the fallen chiefs, to notify to them the royal will, to exercise a general superintendence over them, and especially to guard against and to spy out any conspiracies that might be formed to recover their independence.' And Cruickshank's writing is not the only evidence we have of the Asante system of government. For instance there are records which provide us with the names of the three Asante resident officials posted to Accra in the 1770s, and also those for Abora, Cape Coast and Elmina in the 1810s and 1820s. So we can see that the Asante did certainly make serious attempts to govern, and the fact that their empire lasted so long was due partly to the improved system of their provincial administration. But it was also due, and this was probably the most important factor, to the bravery of their army which enabled them to crush all the insurrections that periodically broke out in the eighteenth and the early part of the nineteenth century.

The political experiment of the Asante was the last and the most successful of the experiments conducted by the Akan. At the turn of the eighteenth century the Asante empire was at the height of its fame and glory. It was easily the greatest and most powerful empire on the west coast of Africa; and it was at the courts of the Asante kings that the culture of the Akan —their language, music, dancing and art—had a chance to flower and develop.

CHAPTER FIVE

The Rise of the Benin Kingdom

Alan Ryder

BY NAME, at least, Benin is probably the best known of all the old West African states. To the European it has been, since the sixteenth century, a symbol of everything which popular imagination and prejudice associated with the equatorial regions of Africa. During the era of partition it won fame by its resistance to the British advance into the interior. More recently, Benin art has had a fruitful influence on western art. In its own African setting, Benin was for many centuries one of the greatest states in the western equatorial region, ruling over a considerable territory to the west of the River Niger.

This kingdom was in many respects an anomaly among the small, unstable chiefdoms of the West African coast. It was the only large centralized state and its capital was the only great city within easy reach of the sea. Yet the basic social structure and customs of Benin were very similar in essentials to those found in the neighbouring, small-scale societies. The Benin people themselves belong to a larger linguistic group known as the Edo-speaking peoples, which is characterized by the same highly localized forms of social and political grouping.

Why then did Benin depart from a political pattern seemingly in harmony with its social structure and suited to its physical environment, a physical environment where the tropical forest hindered the communications that were essential to large-scale organization? Why did Benin set out on a path of

27

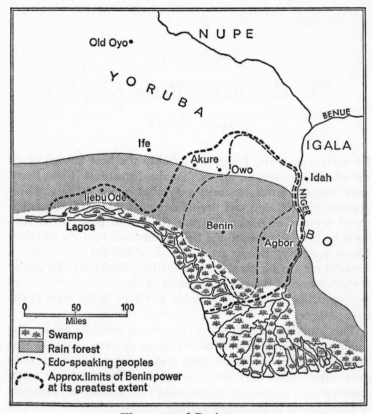

The extent of Benin power

conquest and expansion? Or, to look at the problem from a different point of view, what were the origins of this exceptional state?

Some new light has been thrown on these questions in the past few years by a research project which set out to investigate the history of Benin by studying its language, its social and political institutions, its religion and its art, as well as

28

the rather more obvious historical evidence provided by local oral traditions and European written sources. No final answers can yet be given, because it is clear that they depend on knowing much more than we do at present about other peoples and states of West Africa. But from the evidence we do have it would seem that Benin owed its extraordinary development to three factors: its monarchical traditions, the creation of a complex political and social hierarchy and, arising from these two, the growth of an imperial tradition.

I put the monarchy first, because it was both the mainspring in the functioning of the state and the chief creator of the apparatus of government. The Benin monarchy arose more than six centuries ago, and it had its origins outside Benin. There is a tradition which says that the founder of the dynasty, which still rules today, was Oranmiyan, son of Odudua. He is believed to have come to Benin from Ile-Ife, the original home of the Yoruba people, and to have founded the Oyo dynasty in Yorubaland as well as the royal line of Benin. Similarities between the political institutions of Benin and those of Yoruba kingdoms lend some weight to the belief that they had a common origin. And more support for the tradition comes when we look at the words for political ideas in the Benin and the Yoruba languages. We find that the political vocabularies of the two languages are much more similar than the range of more general words. Yet in spite of this evidence there are still many difficulties in accepting the tradition at its face value; it does not fit in with what we know of the chronology of events in the area. In particular, the Benin dynasty seems to be older than its Yoruba counterparts.

What the stories may represent is the establishment among both peoples of an alien group or dynasty endowed with a reputation for supernatural abilities in the mysteries of government. Dynasties and empires have arisen elsewhere in Africa on such a basis, as among the Mossi, to take an example near at hand. It may be significant that Benin tradition insists that Oranmiyan did not come as a conqueror, but at the invitation of the people who had asked Odudua to send a member of his family to rule them because they were unable to agree among themselves on a system of government. But more must be known about the vanished states on the middle course of the Niger before we can advance beyond speculation on this question.

Wherever its place of origin may have been, the dynastic tie with a foreign overlord for long remained of great importance to the Benin monarchy. Portuguese reports tell us that in the fifteenth century rulers of Benin were still receiving their insignia of office from a spiritual overlord ruling a country farther inland. 'Without these emblems', wrote the Portuguese chronicler De Barros, 'the people would consider that they did not reign lawfully, nor could they call themselves true kings.' Such was the situation some two centuries after the establishment of the dynasty. The link between the kings of Benin and their overlords weakened in the sixteenth century, possibly because something happened to destroy the power or prestige of the latter; but some form of relationship with the senior branch of the dynasty persisted, and we know for certain that in the nineteenth century the ruler of the Yoruba city of Ife was looked upon as a kind of spiritual suzerain by the rulers of Benin. When they died, parts of their bodies were buried in a special cemetery at Ife which is still known in that town as the burial place of the kings of Benin. Excavations have confirmed the existence of the cemetery, but the mean character of the objects found in the graves suggests that the ceremonial attached to them was of a perfunctory kind.

Their relationship to a far-off potentate was one factor which won for the kings of Benin the reverence of their subjects. Another, of still greater importance, was the aura of supernatural power with which they surrounded themselves. The creation of this mystique began with Oranmiyan, who is said to have been accompanied from Ife by a famous practitioner of magic arts. Ewedo, the best known of the early rulers, is remembered as a 'great idolater', who introduced 'various gods' into Benin and instituted numerous ceremonies concerned with worship of the earth spirits and the king's good luck or fortune. The technique of brass-casting by the cire-perdue process also came to Benin from the dynasty's ancestral home, and served to enhance the spiritual authority of the king; for it was by this method—which must have seemed magical to the uninitiated—that the symbols of royal authority and the heads and plaques commemorating the feats of the dynasty were produced.

In course of time, the kings came to lay still greater stress on their supernatural attributes by further elaborating the ritual which surrounded them. This development became most marked from the seventeenth century, when rulers abandoned their function as active military commanders and confined themselves within the palace. In seclusion they devoted much of their time to an increasingly complex routine of religious ceremonial. Human sacrifice grew to the proportions which earned Benin notoriety in the nineteenth century, largely as a result of this emphasis upon the priestly, mystical function of kingship.

But the kingdom of Benin owed its existence over five centuries to something more than the authority and trappings of a semi-divine monarchy. The functioning of the state depended as much, and probably more, upon an elaborate and finely balanced political organization which channelled ambition and ability into its service, while it neutralized conflicts by institutionalizing them. Its essential feature was the association or group of title-holders and aspirants to titles. There were several of these associations, each with a corporate existence and special function within the state. They evolved piecemeal and experimentally over a long period of time; for in Benin there was no sudden transformation of the political structure coinciding with the advent of the dynasty. On the contrary, the successors of Oranmiyan for some time held a precarious position, being obliged to share power with the existing chiefs before they managed to reduce them to the status of one, albeit the senior, titled order. The ruler who thus freed himself from the trammels of the old political system also took the first major step towards the creation of the new by building himself a palace and organizing a hierarchy of household servants and advisers. In so doing, the king, who is said to have been the fourth of his line, was almost certainly following the pattern of government familiar to his dynasty in its ancestral home. Later developments may also have been influenced by the same foreign tradition, but the palace inevitably began to unfold its own needs and potentialities in relation to the new environment, so we must look mainly to the situation within Benin in order to explain the subsequent elaboration of the political system.

According to the traditional reckoning, seven reigns elapsed between the revolution just described and the second major series of political innovations. A new ruler, who had overthrown and murdered his predecessor, consolidated his hold upon Benin by thoroughly remodelling its institutions. His most significant move was the establishment of a new association of titled chiefs sufficiently numerous and influential to balance the powerful palace associations. The circumstances in which he had gained the throne partly explain this seemingly paradoxical action; and one must remember that in Benin as elsewhere organizations, such as the royal household, tended to develop their own vested interests and become the master of those they were created to serve. This ruler found his counter-weight in the men who were prominent in that part of the capital known as the 'town'—that is, those quarters not occupied by the palace, from which they were separated by a broad belt of open land. Many offices and functions of government were assigned to the new order: its senior member, for example, was for long the regular commander of the Benin armies, and its titled chiefs participated with those of the palace in the councils of state which advised the ruler.

In all essentials this was the political structure that governed Benin during the remainder of its independent existence. It endured because it was flexible. With few exceptions, the titles were non-hereditary and in the gift of the ruler, who could also create new ones at his pleasure. In addition the hierarchy was open, at least in theory, to all freeborn men from any part of the kingdom. Thus an able ruler could manipulate the system in such a way as to check over-mighty subjects, balance factions and reward those who served him well.

The close-knit association of monarch and titled orders generated the force which enabled the small city-state of Benin to impose its rule on a great diversity of other peoples, some Edo, some Yoruba and some Ibo. Many submitted in awe of the magical or divine character of the ruler. Others, loosely integrated communities as Benin itself had once been, were overcome by the concentrated power of the autocratic state. A tendency among the subject peoples to copy the political institutions of Benin, especially the title system, and the settlement in some areas of colonists from Benin, introduced an appearance of administrative uniformity in many parts of the Benin dominions. But there was little real unity, and the state remained to the end a heterogeneous empire only held together at the centre by the prestige of the ruler, the watchfulness of the palace and the title-holders, and by the armed might which they could muster against any rebellious town or province.

Thus Benin grew from a small forest town to become the hub of one of the most powerful political systems in West Africa. By the time Europeans first visited Benin at the end of the fifteenth century the structure was already complete, and so well-founded that it survived essentially unchanged through many upheavals for another five hundred years.

CHAPTER SIX

The Impact of the Atlantic Slave Trade on West Africa

Walter Rodney

MANY HISTORIANS have written about the Atlantic slave trade before and, compared with the mass of work on this subject, what I am attempting here can only be a brief summary. But in the past most writers have tended to concentrate on the effect of the slave trade on Europe and the Americas and on the details of how the slaves were actually transported across the Atlantic. More recently research workers have started to look at the available evidence from the point of view of how the slave trade affected Africa. New work on the documents of the period, particularly in Portuguese and Dutch documents, has given us a much fuller picture of the impact of the Atlantic slave trade on well-known centres such as Angola and the Gold Coast. It has also been found that we have to take into account other regions which were previously neglected by students of the slave trade, such as the Upper Guinea Coast.

West African society was not uniform before the coming of Europeans. However, there were fundamental similarities in the patterns of life found in the area bounded by the River Senegal to the north and southern Angola to the south, that is the area which was the principal resort of the European slave ships. In this region society was of course tribal, though the basic social unit was smaller than the tribe; and in some cases there existed what we call 'stateless societies' where there was no political superstructure at all. But for the most part the West African communities constituted states, with territorial boundaries and a ruling class of kings, nobles, elders, priests, clan heads and leaders of secret societies. The rulers were responsible for the order and stability which allowed citizens to get on with their day-to-day lives in peace; they were the guardians of the law and the authorities who decided how land should be used and distributed. In turn, the rulers were supported by the agricultural labour of the majority of the inhabitants. There was also a small amount of manufacturing and exchange by barter. These then were the essentials of the West African culture which was brought into contact with Europe with the coming of the slave trade.

What the West African peoples had in common was even more marked in contrast with the expanding world of mer-cantile capitalism which had its centre in Europe. Given this contrast between West Africa and Europe, it was inevitable that when the two cultures were brought together through trade over a period of several centuries, the impact on West African society would be considerable. This would have been true whatever commodities West Africa supplied to Europe. But the fact was that what European capitalism consistently demanded from Africa was human beings for slaves. The numbers of slaves exported from West Africa have been variously estimated at five million, twelve million, fourteen million and more. Whichever of these figures is nearer the truth, no one would deny that several million West Africans were placed on slave ships or met their deaths as a result of attempts to procure victims for export. This notion of magni-tude is a good enough starting-point, when we try to pick out those changes in West African society which came about because it was human beings which were the object of trade on such a major scale.

Europeans obtained slaves in Africa, on the one hand, by stimulating a demand for the manufactured goods they had to offer, and, on the other hand, by exploiting the tribal and religious divisions and the incipient class contradictions within African society. These features were all involved in the partnership which they established with the ruling hierarchy in the various West African coastal communities.

The consequences of the slave trade for African intertribal and interstate relations have often been discussed in terms of whether wars in the normal course of African affairs readily provided the Europeans with slaves, or whether those wars were not themselves set in motion by the Atlantic slave trade. The fact is that both these interpretations have some truth in them. There were instances when European ships obtained slaves as an incidental by-product of wars fought by the Africans, particularly during the early years of the slave trade. There were occasions when the outbreak of hostilities could be attributed to nothing but the presence of slave-buying Europeans and the lure of European manufactures. In general, however, it seems clear that the prospects of profit from the slave trade became so attractive that old rivalries were either revived or smoothed over, according to which was the most profitable.

By the height of the Atlantic slave trade in the eighteenth century the procurement of captives for sale had become the principal motivation for an endless succession of intergroup conflicts on the West African coast. Occasionally the pattern of political power in an area was decisively affected by the influence of the slave trade. The kingdom of Kongo-Angola is the classic example of a West African state whose structure and coherence were destroyed by the intensity of the slave trade as pursued by the Portuguese and their local mulatto mercenaries. The Yoruba political federation also disintegrated in the face of slave raiding by its African neighbours. On the other hand, states like Dahomey, Asante and the Futa Djalon increased their power while acting as agents of the Atlantic slave trade. In this way, then, the slave trade influenced different areas in different ways.

It is equally important to assess the manner in which slave raiding affected people at different social levels within the hierarchical society of West Africa. For the vast majority it brought insecurity and fear, whether or not they were lucky enough to escape sale into slavery, because the slave trade meant violence in the form of skirmishes, ambushes and kidnapping—often carried out by professional man-hunters, under the supervision of the ruling elites. This atmosphere of fear caused people to flee from their villages into the bush or remove their homes to places which were difficult to get to and agriculturally inhospitable. Alternatively, as was noticeable on the waterside, many Africans walked in armed expectation of attack.

But there was one section of the African community which was, to a large extent, immune from the perils of the slave trade. This was the ruling class. For many members of the ruling class were engaged in a partnership of exploitation with the Europeans and, by a variety of devices, they protected themselves from being captured, sold to the slavers and exported. Furthermore the ruling class took advantage of their legal authority to classify people as 'criminals' and have them sold. For instance it was easy enough to bring trumped-up charges of adultery against perfectly innocent people. Not only had the ruling classes ceased to administer the customary law in a spirit of justice, but the law itself became thoroughly debased. Reports on West African penal codes in the sixteenth and seventeenth centuries show that there was a system of mild penalties, usually involving the payment of damages to the aggrieved party. And yet in the period of the Atlantic slave trade a punishment as drastic as sale into slavery was introduced for a larger and larger number of offences, descending right down to the most trivial. In effect the common people had lost the security of person which the customary law had guaranteed them in the past; while once more the ruling classes were well protected.

However, the African allies of the Europeans in any given society were not necessarily the same throughout the period of the Atlantic slave trade. This was because the traditional ruling classes did not always escape the upheavals which they themselves had set in motion. Possibly because they were not sufficiently ruthless, and certainly because they were not commercially equipped to meet the requirements of the slave ships, many of the old ruling groups found themselves replaced. And they were replaced by a new class of men who owed their strength to the skill and devotion with which they served the capitalist system. Sometimes, as on the old Gold Coast and around the Niger Delta, the new elite was drawn from within local society. But more often, as on the Upper Guinea Coast and in nineteenth-century Dahomey, they were professional slave traders of part-European origin: Afro-Portuguese, Afro-English and Afro-Brazilian.

Apart from these changes at leadership level, the status of many common people became depressed and the division of society into different classes became more rigid. Even at the time when the first Europeans arrived, certain members of the communities on the West African Coast had only limited freedom. In the fifteenth century, particularly in the larger states and more complex societies which had arisen outside the forest belt, numbers of domestic servants without privileges, serfs and chattel slaves were found. Active involvement in the Atlantic slave trade invariably meant the increase of such servile categories in the societies where they existed, and their creation where they had not previously existed. Thus it was that by the end of the eighteenth century a sizeable proportion of the inhabitants of West Africa found themselves under some sort of servitude. Indeed well into the present century major slave-raiding groups, like the Fulas of the Futa Djalon and the Nike of Eastern Nigeria, still kept a large labour force in conditions of bondage.

When we move from political and social structure to other spheres of West African life, it is rather more difficult to pin down the effects of the Atlantic slave trade. As far as religion is concerned, for instance, the most that can be said with assurance is that the priests were usually involved on the side of the slave traders, along with powerful spiritual institutions such as secret societies. Religious authorities were adept at uncovering instances of witchcraft which meant that the accused were sold to the Europeans. There was obvious chicanery in these procedures, although the practice of witch-craft may have increased under the disturbed social conditions of the slave-trade era. Another area of darkness is that of moral values. Some African chiefs were frank in admitting that they recognized the inhumanity of the slave trade, but had consciously abandoned moral precept in favour of the loot, which was measured in yards of cloth and gallons of alcohol. The presumption is strong that only through a weakening in the moral fibre of the society as a whole could Africans have come to co-operate in the large-scale trafficking in their own kind, though it is improbable that historical evidence could be produced to signpost the devious downhill route which was followed.

Curiously enough, in spite of the fact that the slave trade was primarily an economic phenomenon, it is by no means easy to discern its effect on the West African economy. Most of the assertions must be negative ones. The trade certainly did not stimulate any productive resources in Africa, as it did in Europe and the New World. On the contrary it distracted efforts away from agriculture and manufactures. The intro-duction of European goods in itself brought no economic benefits, since the goods were consumed without creating growth in the economy.

In attempting an overall assessment of the significance of the Atlantic slave trade it is useful to try to answer this question which is currently being raised: 'Was the Atlantic slave trade entirely destructive of African society?' On the one hand, values, individual security and freedom, traditional social relations and some social units were all undermined, while the economy stagnated and human resources were wasted. On the other hand some social and ethnic groups grew more powerful and the very extension of servile con-ditions within West Africa strengthened the position of other sectors of the society. Even these positive consequences confirm that the Atlantic slave trade eroded the old order in West Africa. But they do mean that we have to qualify the notion of the slave trade as a bush fire which left nothing standing. What mattered most for the area was its survival as a viable society. In the first place the haemorrhage of population was not fatal, and the region remained in the possession of the indigenous peoples. In the second place, in spite of the experiences of the slave trade West Africa continued to be part of the global system of production. Indeed the demand for European goods which first led West Africans to participate in the slave trade in the fifteenth century, had become more and more insistent as Africans came to regard manufactures as necessities. This demand was the stimulus for new experiments in West Africa in the late nineteenth and in the early twentieth century.

CHAPTER SEVEN

Dating the African Past

J. R. Gray

IN ANY HISTORICAL ANALYSIS, just as in telling a good story, the elementary, but essential, task is to place the events in their right order. Without a chronological sequence, a historian cannot be certain whether he is dealing with cause or effect. Yet, fifteen years ago, when I was beginning my apprenticeship as a historian, few if any scholars believed that it would ever be possible to reconstruct a detailed chronology for the history of tropical Africa. Only on the edges of this vast area—in the Sudanese belt, in Ethiopia and on the coastal fringe of East Africa—had Africans produced a thin, uncertain skeleton of documentary evidence. Without indigenous, contemporary records the chances of arriving at a fixed sequence of events seemed intimidatingly slender.

In dating their sites archaeologists had still in those days to rely mainly on finding imported objects. But sites where there was a significant number of imported objects which could be identified and dated were relatively few. Elsewhere imported relics were generally limited to a few beads, which are notoriously difficult to date, while many sites of great importance have produced no imported evidence at all. It was already clear that, for a few favoured areas, the king-lists recorded in oral traditions could yield some indication of the period spanned by a particular dynasty. But historians were only beginning to exploit this line of inquiry, and in the general absence of fixed dates an often spurious chronology tended to be reproduced uncritically or, at best, apologetically.

For archaeologists, dating has been revolutionized during the past fifteen years by the development of radiocarbon analysis. It is now theoretically possible to analyse the remains of any piece of organic matter, whether animal or vegetable, and to say how long ago it died. The method is expensive, and many technical problems have had to be overcome in applying it. But the experimental period is now almost over, and the results produced so far make sense. They are broadly consistent with one another, and they are not inconsistent with other kinds of evidence.

For the Iron Age in Africa, that is, for the period from about 500 B.C. onwards, there are now more than one hundred carbon dates. For such a large area, this is a pathetically small number, but even so it has already sharpened the focus of African history, and for Zambia and Rhodesia, where about half the available dates are concentrated, the outlines of a chronology are becoming apparent. We now know that the knowledge of iron working, which had spread into the Nile valley by about the fifth century B.C., had reached Northern Nigeria by the third century B.C. and the Zambezi region about three centuries later. We also know that the distinctive and widespread style of pottery decoration, which occurs in the earliest Iron Age levels throughout eastern and central Africa, was being carried outwards, north and south, from the Zambezi during the first half of the first millennium.

Carbon dating is also establishing an exciting, and at times surprising, sequence for later developments in central Africa. The great site of Zimbabwe in Rhodesia, with some of the most impressive historical buildings in tropical Africa, has yet to be fully dated; but the results so far obtained, with a consistent development from the fourth century A.D. to an eleventh-century date just before the beginning of stone building, have fully vindicated the few scholarly archaeologists who had previously maintained that the builders were Iron Age Africans.

The greatest surprises, however, which carbon dating has

so far provided have been the eighth- and ninth-century dates for an immense cemetery at Lake Kisale in the Katanga and for a trading site on the upper Zambezi at Ingombe Ilede. These dates have opened up completely new horizons, shifting interest inwards to the energies generated at the heart of Bantu-speaking Africa; for they show that a highly sophisticated culture, similar to that associated with the later periods of Zimbabwe, was already flourishing in the far interior some five hundred years earlier than had previously been suspected.

So far these results stand by themselves. Nowhere else in sub-Saharan Africa is there even a tentative sequence. But this should soon change. An international conference of African archaeologists and historians, convened by the School of Oriental and African Studies of the University of London in July 1966, agreed that carbon dating could bring an immense contribution to the study of African history. It considered that during the next five years something like a thousand new carbon dates might be expected from African Iron Age sites, and that a systematic programme of dating would provide an indispensable framework for the solution of some of the outstanding problems of early African history.

For the last four or five hundred years of African history radiocarbon dating is far less important. This is because its accuracy declines appreciably as one approaches the present day, making any date later than about 1600 unreliable. For most of non-literate Africa its place is taken from here onwards by oral traditions. Here again during the last decade significant advances have been made, not merely in the use of this evidence, but specifically in refining its chronology. The accurate preservation of dynastic histories has often been a matter of life or death—a lapse of memory, a lapse on the part of one of the custodians could sometimes lead to execution. The recollection of reigns and generations is therefore of a remarkable reliability and distortions can generally be detected; but there is often no other ready indication of the time-depth involved. Even in the case of peoples who have had literate scribes for several centuries, such as the Hausa states in Northern Nigeria, the chronology of the chronicles, which incorporate traditions, is in places seriously imperfect.

In these circumstances the search for a fixed date which can be referred to a point in the traditional genealogy is obviously of supreme importance. The scrutiny of the records of European traders and missionaries from the fifteenth century onwards is already yielding results; for although these reports are mainly confined to the coastal fringe, the linkage, as Dr David Birmingham has shown (see page 58), with the peoples of west central Africa, can sometimes be extended far into the interior. The encounters of shipwrecked sailors on the coast of South Africa provide several fixed points for the south-eastern Bantu; and Asante chronology has been clarified by trading records from the Gold Coast. Turkish and Arabic material from North Africa strengthens the chronology of the Sudanic states; in turn the chronicles and manuscripts of these states, many of which are only now being studied, provide a network of references deep into the forest fringes; while Swahili and Arabic documentation from the Indian Ocean coast may yet play an important role in East African chronology.

Astronomy can also play a part. Over fifty years ago, Torday, recording the history of the Bushoong people in the Congo, was startled by the casual remark that, during the reign of one king, 'one day at noon the sun went out, and there was absolute darkness for a short time'. He identified this with the total eclipse of 1680, and other evidence makes it fairly certain that his identification is correct. About thirty-five years ago another example was identified: the crossing of the Zambezi by the Ngoni migrants from Zululand during the total eclipse of 1835.

During 1966 a series of large-scale maps showing the paths of eclipses in Africa has been drawn. The quite new degree of accuracy obtained in these maps gives the historian a tool with which he can begin the task of identifying a reference to an eclipse in tradition. The probabilities can be clarified by further calculations, so that in a few cases the identification can be regarded as virtually certain, providing a fixed date of great precision. For example, the new maps have suggested that we should make some important corrections to our ideas of the early chronology of the Hausa states; they have solved a minor problem in the early nineteenth-century history of the northern Transvaal; they have strengthened a reconstruction of Lunda chronology on the upper Zambezi; they have confirmed that the eclipse seen by the Kabaka Juko in Buganda was almost certainly that of 1680; they strongly indicate that the celebrated eclipse which occurred at Biharwe in Uganda during the reign of the fifth Mukama of Bunyoro is to be identified with a total eclipse of 1520.

Fixed dates, obtained either from the heavens or from the more usual, documentary evidence handled by historians, are of crucial importance, not only for the particular dynasty in which they occur, but also because, through cross references, they can often establish the chronology of a far wider area. The Ngoni crossing of the Zambezi had repercussions throughout eastern and central Africa, and the eclipse at Biharwe may provide a fixed date for all the major dynasties of Uganda, north-western Tanzania, Rwanda, Burundi and parts of the eastern Congo. Asante chronology has implications for most of the Akan states, and there are relatively few areas in West Africa which are not reached by cross references, moving inwards in a chain reaction from points established by either the coastal or Sudanic documentation.

As traditional material is studied and collected it is becoming increasingly evident that here also the archaeologist has a vital, if subsidiary, role. Many capitals, trading centres, sacred groves and other sites of historic importance are remembered accurately in tradition. With sites such as the great earthwork capital site at Bigo in western Uganda, which is connected in oral tradition with the earliest remembered dynasty, radiocarbon dating may still provide an accurate and invaluable baseline. Nearer the present, the archaeological sequence can check traditions, and it may well clarify processes such as the arrival of Islam and the development of urbanization.

There are of course large areas and periods whose chronology remains at best relative, and which cannot as yet be fixed within anything like an absolute framework. Yet even in these cases the S.O.A.S. Conference in July 1966 made it clear that historians are discovering an increasing range of evidence which can be made to yield chronological information. The crude calculation of dynastic time, by taking an average length for a generation or even a reign, can sometimes be considerably refined by attention to the modes of succession, fertility indices and factors influencing a particular society. The possibility of providing internal cross checks is also by no means restricted to cross references between dynastic lists. Even in stateless societies the sequences of ritual leaders, and the lineages and settlement patterns of ordinary people can supply chronological evidence, and, when dealing with states, this promising line of inquiry can be used to supplement the bare skeleton of a dynastic list.

We stand merely on the threshold of this search. The radiocarbon dating of Iron Age Africa is still in its infancy. The sources for fixed dates are only now being thoroughly exploited. Yet already historians can begin to glimpse the possibility of a reliable chronology for many of the major historical developments of tropical Africa.

CHAPTER EIGHT

The Impact of the Nilotes

Bethwell Ogot

THE FORMATION of most of the East African societies which exist today took place between 1400 and 1900. The main factor in their evolution was the continuous flow of migration and conquest within the continent. Migrations into and within East Africa led to new encounters, new ideas were diffused and dispersed along the migration routes, and cultural forms were transplanted from one region to another. The result of all this movement was the evolution of larger and more integrated societies with more complex social institutions.

One of the most important movements of peoples during this period was that of the Nilotes. Today they number about four million, and are represented in the north by the Shilluk of the White Nile, the Dinka, the Nuer, the Anywak who extend into Ethiopia, and other smaller groups such as the Atwot, the Pari, the Bor, the Luo of Wau, and others. The central bloc of Nilotes, the majority of whom live in northern Uganda, consist of the Acholi, the Lango and the Alur, who stretch into the Oriental Province of the Republic of Congo, and the Palwo, who form a small group in the north-eastern corner of Bunyoro. Finally, we have the southern Nilotes, consisting of the Padhola who live in eastern Uganda, and the Kenya Luo who spill over into the Musoma district of Tanzania.

It is generally accepted that by about A.D. 1000, the Nilotes had emerged as a distinct group in the south-eastern part

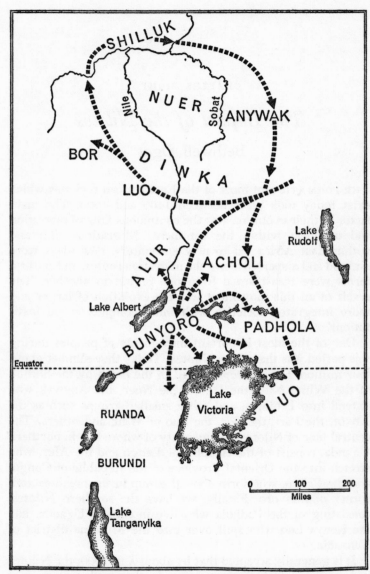

Approximate movements of the Nilotes

48

of the Republic of Sudan. These early Nilotes were mainly pastoral and nomadic, living by their flocks. Their political organization was rudimentary, the society being held together through kinship ties.

In a series of major waves of migration which started between 1200 and 1500, and which continued for another four centuries after 1500, the Nilotes scattered northwards to occupy the Bahr-el-Ghazal and Malakal areas of Sudan, eastwards into Ethiopia, westwards into eastern Congo, and southwards into Uganda, Kenya and Tanzania. They found themselves living amongst a vast variety of peoples—Sudanic, Bantu and 'Nilo-Hamitic'. In many of these areas, they formed a ruling minority of conquerors and rulers; and when this happened the Nilotes imposed their languages upon the previous populations. It appears from traditional evidence that the major impulse behind the migrations must have been land hunger. The early Nilotes were driven by the pressure of overpopulation in their original home to seek an outlet in the neighbouring regions and, since they were successful colonists, their populations continued to increase rapidly in all the widely dispersed places where they settled.

The first of the Nilotes to move were the Dinka and the Nuer, who claim to be descended from a common ancestor. According to their tradition, they moved only a short distance from their original home. And it seems that they moved into country that was nearly empty. For instance, if we look at the relationship between groups of the Dinka tribe living in different areas we do not find that some groups are dominant and others less important in the structure of the tribe. Nor do they distinguish between 'the owners of the soil' and 'the late-comers' or 'stranger lineages'. This is perhaps because they did not absorb any aliens. Up to the present, the Dinka lineages are not bound together by territorial unity. 'The basis of their unity', Dr Godfrey Lienhardt has written, 'is less the occupation of particular settled territories than the exploitation and defence of particular pastures, by their members, in the wet and dry seasons.' In the case of the Nuer, although there are dominant clans, we find that the other clans grafted on to them were either Nuer or Dinka. We therefore see that the kind of prolonged and fruitful inter- action which occurred between the incoming pastoralists and the local agriculturists in the lake region of Uganda was absent in the Sudan—at least amongst the Dinka and the Nuer.

Farther north, on the White Nile, another Nilotic group, the Shilluk, successfully imposed their rule over people of diverse origin. The original party of Nyikango, the founder of Shilluk society, was small. Today they are represented by two major groups: the Kwar Reth and the Ororo. The small Nilotic party absorbed many stranger elements *en route*; and on their arrival in Fashoda they conquered other populations, most of whom they eventually assimilated.

The Shilluk society was established during the first half of the sixteenth century. Under the able leadership of Nyi- kango, the different peoples were gradually welded together into a strong nation; and by the end of the seventeenth century, the Shilluk Rethship in its complex form was already established.

It is possible that there was a relationship between the Shilluk and the Fung dynasty, which ruled most of the north- ern Sudan from the sixteenth century till the early nineteenth century. James Bruce was the first writer to assert, in 1770, that the Fung were of Shilluk origin. Since then, other writers such as Westermann and Arkell have produced further evi- dence in defence of Bruce's theory. Arkell, for instance, has summarized the theory in the following way. The Fung were not a tribe, but a group of invaders, the northernmost wave of a great Shilluk upheaval on the White Nile, that reached the Blue Nile, just when the Arabs were beginning to overrun the southernmost Christian kingdom of Nubia, that of Aloa. These Shilluk provided a new dynasty for Aloa, and having much in common with its inhabitants, due to a common inheritance from ancient Egypt, they led them against the Arabs, defeating them in battle and forcing them to pay tribute.

But since it was a time when Islam was in the ascendant, and when the Ottoman Turks were threatening invasion from Egypt and the Red Sea ports, the Fung then became Muslims, invented a pedigree claiming descent from the Prophet and pretended that their ancestor had come from the Hejaz via Abyssinia. As a small conquering group, they soon forgot the Shilluk language and adopted Arabic, which was, no doubt, already beginning to spread among their subjects.

If this is indeed the true story of the Fung, it could be compared with the fortunes of another Nilotic group, the Bito, who provided a new dynasty for Bunyoro-Kitara, incorporating the traditions of the earlier Chwezi dynasty into their own traditions and adopting the Bantu tongue of the conquered majority.

At the same time that the Shilluk kingdom was being established, a Nilotic settlement was founded along the Sobat River by a migration from the Wipac area of Luo-speaking elements supposed to be closely related to the Shilluk. These are the people who today are known as the Anywak. They evolved a kingship system similar to that of the Shilluk, but simpler in form; and in south-eastern Anywakland, the power and prestige of the kingship was later extended considerably, with the help of Ethiopian muskets.

However, it is in present-day Uganda that the Nilotes made their greatest impact. In order to assess the quality of this impact, we should distinguish between the western and southern parts of Uganda and the northern and eastern sections. In the western and southern areas there were settled agricultural societies by 1500 when the Luo-speakers arrived. These populous areas around Lake Victoria had already acted as a shock-absorber for other pastoral incursions, and although the invaders had afterwards formed ruling groups, these were always in the end assimilated into the Bantu majority. At the time of the Luo invasion the largest state in this area was called Kitara and it was ruled by a dynasty called the Bachwezi. Politically, the arrival of the Luo-speakers in Uganda was an epoch-making event. They displaced the Bachwezi rulers of the Kitara empire and founded several related Bito kingdoms such as Bunyoro, Buganda, Koki, Kiziba, Toro and the principalities of northern Busoga. Under their rule, the former Chwezi dominions have been consolidated and expanded.

In these new Bito states there does not seem to have been any hostility between the ruling minority and their subjects. Because they assimilated the Luo minority, the Bantu societies showed no hostility to the impact of Nilotic culture. As a result, a new culture gradually developed in the Bito kingdoms, which was a synthesis of Bantu and Nilotic elements.

The political impact of the Nilotes extended well beyond the old Kitara empire. In response to Luo pressure, the Bahima, the old pastoral ruling class, had withdrawn *en masse* southwards into Ankole, Karagwe and Ruanda, where they established new dynasties.

In contrast with the southern part, eastern and northern Uganda were sparsely populated at the time of the Luo invasions. Here the Luo were the initiators, not the inheritors, of the political system. The best example of this assimilative power of Nilotic culture is seen in Alurland, where it operated in two ways. In the highlands the Atyak and Ucibu clans, who reached the area about fourteen generations ago, brought a wide area and a large number of diverse peoples under their sway by planting out chieflets from existing Luo chiefships to rule non-Luo groups.

At the same time, in the lowlands of the Alur country the Luo were extending their influence in another way. Here most of the Luo chieflets came from the great Bito state of Bunyoro, though they claimed no agnatic kinship with the

Bito dynasty. Theirs was a political claim based on regalia and other emblems of chiefship. Once the chieflets had obtained the approval of the Bito rulers of Bunyoro, they did not expand their territories by planting out their sons among non-Luo populations as the highland chiefs were doing. Instead they gave political authority to certain favoured or chiefly clan heads who then ruled over Luo and non-Luo elements.

Some of the Acholi chiefs were planted out in this way from Pawir, the Luo-speaking part of Bunyoro, and should therefore be compared with the Alur chieflets. The leaders of these Palwo clans established themselves, apparently without fighting, as rulers amongst the Moru-Madi groups who spoke Sudanic languages. The lowlands of Alurland and the regions of Acholiland colonized by Palwo clans should thus be regarded as the last outposts of Bunyoro. In this way new Luo societies were gradually created out of heterogeneous elements.

In the rest of Acholiland, in the modern Lango district and in eastern Uganda, the Luo immigrants were responsible for the creation of new communities out of mixed groups. For example according to a survey conducted by Dr Girling, 43 per cent of Acholi clans claim origin from the Luo, 17 per cent from the Karamojong, 14 per cent from the Lango, 9 per cent from the Madi, 2 per cent from the Bari, and the rest are miscellaneous. Most of the Acholi 'royal lineages', the *lokal* or *lokeer* or *lobito* are of Luo derivation, whereas the commoner clans—the *bon* or *lobon* or simply *lwak* (the mass)—were originally non-Luo. It would appear therefore that the Acholi society was formed of various people settling down in one territory under Luo leadership, taking up a common economic life of pastoralism and rudimentary agriculture, and in the course of time speaking a common Acholi language and evolving a common Acholi culture, so that ultimately they considered themselves only as Acholi. The true wonder of Nilotic expansion in Uganda was thus their cultural assimilation of the conquered provinces rather than their original military prowess.

It should also be evident from what we have said that the foundations of Uganda lie deeper than the establishment of British administration in the territory. The notion of Uganda as a unity may be traced back to the Bachwezi overrule established in most parts of Uganda some time in the fifteenth century. This overrule was consolidated under the Luo Babito, who succeeded the Bachwezi as the rulers of Bunyoro-Kitara. And from the seventeenth century to the middle of the nineteenth century, the history of most parts of Uganda is largely the history of Bunyoro and her satellite states, of which Buganda eventually emerged as the pre-eminent power. So that when the British took over in 1894, Uganda, unlike Kenya, was not simply a geographical expression. Several attempts, some more successful than others, had been made to administer the whole area as a unit. In all these attempts, the Nilotic factor was important.

The largest group of the Nilotes, however, are the Kenya Luo, who live mainly in south and central Nyanza districts. Although they are the only Nilotes in Kenya, their migrations and settlement made a significant impact on the human geography of the lake basin. They imposed their language and culture on a large number of Bantu and 'Nilo-Hamitic' peoples, most of whom were eventually assimilated. This cultural influence extended even to areas such as Buluyia and Gusii which, strictly speaking, are outside the Nilotic zone of influence.

Another important consequence of the Luo invasion of the lake region of Kenya is that it forced the different and warring Luyia clans to unite, and thereby accelerated the evolution of bigger and more complex societies. The same applied to the Gusii, although to a lesser degree.

To sum up, on one hand a major result of the great dispersion of the Nilotes was that in those areas with great density of population state formation became the distinguishing feature associated with their incursion. Another major result, on the other hand, was that in sparsely populated regions, the advent of the Nilotes led to the creation of new and bigger societies from diverse elements.

CHAPTER NINE

Central Africa and the Atlantic Slave Trade

David Birmingham

THE WESTERN PORTION OF CENTRAL AFRICA is a region of light woodland intersected by many rivers; it lies between the equatorial forest of the Congo and the arid scrubland of the Kalahari Desert. Until the fifteenth century this pleasant part of Africa remained a backwater. Its inhabitants lived beyond the reach of world trade. In this they were quite unlike the people of West Africa, who had long maintained thriving commercial contacts with the Mediterranean, or those of East Africa who were linked to the monsoon trading system of the Indian Ocean. These isolated peoples of west central Africa consisted mainly of western Bantu-speaking groups who had migrated into the area over the course of the previous thousand years. They were in fact the westernmost representatives of the great family of Bantu-speaking peoples, which today occupies most of Africa south of the equator. When, in the late fifteenth century, central Africa came into commercial contact with the outside world, two groups of western Bantu peoples came to play an especially important historical role. These were the Mbundu and the Lunda.

Some close parallels can be drawn between the Mbundu and the Lunda peoples. Both were nations of simple peasant farmers. They grew millet and bananas and reared small livestock. The Mbundu also traded in salt and the Lunda were noted experts at fishing and hunting. Until the fifteenth century neither the Mbundu nor the Lunda had a strong or centralized government. From then onwards both began to adopt ideas about kingship from their more powerful neighbours. The Mbundu, who lived on the southern fringe of the great kingdom of Kongo, gradually built up the small kingdom of Angola. The Lunda, whose territory lay several hundred miles farther into the interior, acquired their ideas of

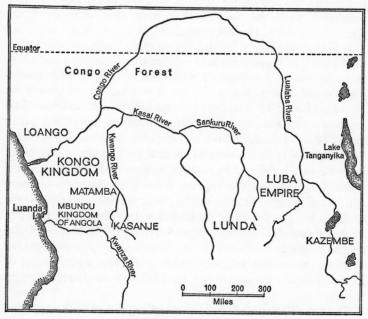

West Central Africa

military and political organization from the complex empire of their Luba neighbours, who lived in the northern part of the Katanga region.

The first contact between the peoples of west central Africa and the outside world came in the 1480s, when Portuguese seafarers reached the shores of Angola and met the

Mbundu. This meeting is still remembered in the local folk-lore. The white men arrived in ships with wings which shone in the sun like knives; they brought maize and cassava and groundnuts and tobacco; they said prayers to the Holy Father and to the Son in order that the new crops might prosper; they exchanged cloth and beads for eggs and chickens. But the white men also brought trouble; they spat fire from guns and captured the king's salt pans. The tradition concludes with the lament that from that time until the present day the whites brought nothing but wars and miseries.

It is possible today for the historian to begin to reconstruct the history of these wars and miseries and examine the long-term effects which contact with the outside world had on the peoples of west central Africa. For this reconstruction the historian has at his disposal two main types of evidence. The internal evidence consists of the oral chronicles of the many states of west central Africa. This oral evidence, describing how the people see themselves and their history, can in some cases be supplemented by outside evidence of how others saw them. In particular the written records of Portuguese trade and warfare give extra detail and precise dating to the western fringe of central African history. These two types of evidence usefully complement each other; the weakness of oral tradition is that its dating is based on such imprecise concepts as generations and reign-lengths, while the shortcoming of European records is that they tend to over-emphasize foreign enterprise.

The first Portuguese to follow the explorers to Angola and make contact with the Mbundu were traders who came to buy slaves. These slaves were needed in many parts of the Portuguese empire. They were used to plant sugar on the island of São Tomé, to exchange for gold dust on the Gold Coast, to replenish the diminished supply of labour in Portugal itself and, most important of all, to colonize the new lands in Brazil. When the traders first made contact with the king of Angola, at the beginning of the sixteenth century, they found him to be only a minor ruler. The opening of the slave trade, however, soon furnished him with a sharp incentive to territorial expansion. By conducting wars and raids on his neighbours, the king of Angola could capture prisoners for sale on the coast. The European manufactures which he gained in return then further increased his wealth and prestige, thus attracting new followers and giving him the power to conduct yet greater expansionist campaigns. By mid-century Angola had become sufficiently important to attract the official interest of the Portuguese crown.

In the past, when they had been dealing with the kingdom of Kongo, the Portuguese had attempted a policy of partnership with the African kings they contacted. They came under considerable pressure to drop this policy when they turned their attention to Angola. At home in Portgual economic and colonial advisers recommended the use of force to impose a lasting Portuguese government on Angola. These advisers were influenced in this attitude by the newly founded Society of Jesus. After an abortive attempt at a peaceful conversion, the Jesuit missionaries interested in Angola became convinced that Christianity could only be effectively propagated in a country which was governed by a powerful Christian government. This Portuguese attitude was reinforced by the behaviour of the Angolan king. He received diplomatic missions sent to him from Portugal with circumspection verging on hostility. In two cases he went so far as to detain the leaders of Portuguese delegations for several years. By 1571 the combined effects of pressure from the militant lobby in Portugal and failure of diplomatic initiatives in Angola led the impetuous young Sebastian of Portugal to approve a plan for the military conquest of Angola.

This Portuguese decision to conquer Angola marks the end of the first century of Angolan contact with the outside world. During that century the country had grown and its economy had been stimulated by participation in the slave trade. Thereafter, when Angola began its conflict with Portugal, it entered upon a century of decline in which the king's power was eroded and finally destroyed. During the wars the relationship between the Portuguese and the ruler of Angola was a complex and fluctuating one. In one season they would be at war and in the next they would be trading together in a mutually beneficial exchange of slaves for alcohol, tobacco and clothing. When the Portuguese finally destroyed Angola and forced the reigning queen to flee, they hoped that they would gain new strength and an improved commercial position. They soon found out, however, that this was not the case. They realized too late that their position depended on having a satisfactory trading partner, even one who was intermittently hostile to their intentions. Having destroyed the Angolan monarchy they therefore had to set to and search for a new trading partner. They eventually made contact with the same Mbundu queen whom they had driven out of Angola only a few years earlier. After her defeat Queen Nzinga had retired two hundred miles from the coast and formed a new kingdom of Mbundu refugees called Matamba. During the seventeenth century Matamba expanded its trade with the Portuguese and became far more important to them than the puppet kingdom which they had painstakingly established in Angola after nearly a century of warfare.

The long wars which led to the destruction of Angola and the rise of Matamba caused a great upheaval, the repercussions of which spread out in ripples over west central Africa until they affected the Lunda people in the heart of the continent. I have already mentioned the Lunda and explained that during the sixteenth century they were undergoing fundamental political changes as they began to develop ideas of a more centralized system of government taken from their neighbours. During the course of these changes dissident groups broke away and migrated to the west. One of these groups settled near the Portuguese territory and began to take part in the slave trade. These Lunda immigrants established a trading kingdom called Kasanje, which was strategically placed just outside the range of the Portuguese armies. During the seventeenth century Kasanje and Matamba became the main rivals attempting to control the trade routes and slave centres of west central Africa.

By the eighteenth century the Kasanje slave trade had begun to have a marked influence on the emerging Lunda empire. As the new empire gained in strength and administrative complexity, it expanded its territories and fostered satellite states through which to control its commercial interests. Some of these states were established in the western part of the empire to facilitate direct Lunda participation in the Atlantic slave trade. This trade thus evolved in three tiers: Angola and the coastal region, now drastically reduced in population, was controlled by the Portuguese; central Africa, which became the main source of slaves, was controlled by the Lunda, and in between lay the small states of Kasanje and Matamba, which acted as middlemen between the suppliers and the purchasers. This position of middleman, acting both as a barrier and a link in the supply routes of the slave trade, was a common one in Africa, but only in Angola were the intermediate states so far from the coast; in West Africa the Europeans were restricted to small enclaves around their forts and the middlemen developed their states in the immediate interior.

As the Lunda empire grew, the emperor—called the Mwata Yamvo—began to seek means of diversifying the basis of his power. The initial economic stimulus to imperial expansion had come in the seventeenth century from selling slaves through Kasanje to the Portuguese. In the eighteenth century the Lunda spread out in a north-westerly direction and began to trade with the English, French and Dutch on the coast north of the Congo River. During the same period the Lunda rulers began to seek new trading opportunities in the east. They founded the Kazembe kingdom, which gained control of part of the lucrative ivory trade directed towards the Indian Ocean. Thus by the end of the eighteenth century the Lunda emperor held a grip on a large share of the trade of central Africa and could use his own economic judgement in deciding whether to direct commodities to the Portuguese in Angola or to the North Europeans on the Congo or to the Muslim traders in the Indian Ocean.

One can thus see that from the fifteenth to the eighteenth centuries there was a chain of influence beginning with the opening of the Angolan coast to overseas trade. In the sixteenth century the trade stimulated the growth of the kingdom of Angola. One stage later, in the seventeenth century, Angola decayed and disappeared, while Kasanje and Matamba rose to prominence in the hinterland. In the last phase of growth in the Atlantic slave trade, during the eighteenth century, Kasanje and Matamba were gradually overshadowed by the mighty empire of Lunda, which eventually far surpassed them in both economic and political power.

But it would be misleading to end this account on a note of political achievement. The historian can examine the skill with which the Lunda and other central African rulers made political use of the new economic circumstances deriving from contact with the outside world. He must also, however, look at the fate of the ordinary people and remember the lament of the Mbundu who said that the white men brought nothing but wars and miseries. The introduction of long-distance trade stimulated the growth of states, but it also increased the dangers and uncertainties of everyday life. The number of slaves taken from central Africa to the New World may have amounted to four million people and countless millions of others lived their entire lives in fear and uncertainty owing to the arrival of European traders on the shores of their homeland.

CHAPTER TEN

The History of the Bemba

Andrew Roberts

THE BEMBA OF NORTH-EASTERN ZAMBIA are among the best-known peoples of central Africa. Livingstone travelled through their country in the course of his last expedition. In the late nineteenth century, the Bemba became notorious as slave raiders. Today, the Bemba are known as strong and daring workers in the mines of the Copperbelt. They provide much of the leadership and support for the nationalist movement which in 1964 obtained Zambia's independence from British rule.

This prominence of the Bemba is reflected in numerous detailed studies of their economic and social life. By comparison, their history has been rather neglected. I therefore thought it worth while to compare a few written records with what the Bemba themselves remember today about their past. In 1964 and 1965 I spent a year travelling in and around Bemba country, seeking out people who in one way or another had an interest in preserving historical traditions. Such people, in all societies, are often connected with the business of government, which always has need of history to furnish precedents. So I first turned my attention to the Bemba political system.

In pre-colonial days, all the peoples in north-eastern Zambia were ruled by hereditary chiefs. Each chief had a territory of his own, and the more important ones had a number of hereditary councillors who determined chiefly succession and supervised chiefly rituals. It was the business

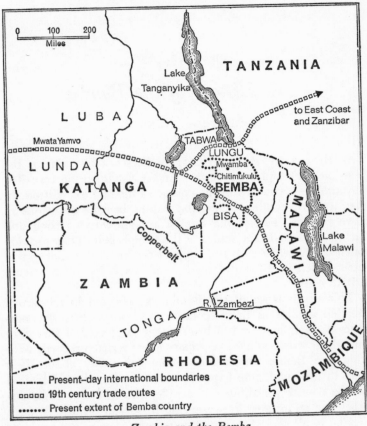

Zambia and the Bemba

of such councillors to explain the origins of chieftainships and to keep some record of the fortunes of different chiefly families. In modern times, the powers of chiefs have been greatly reduced, and the migration of able-bodied men to work for long periods in the towns has interfered with the transmission of oral traditions. But some of the customs of chieftainship survive, in particular the traditional rules for selecting chiefs. And it is still possible—though it may not be for much longer—to find old men who can fulfil their appointed roles as court historians.

My first problem, then, was to find the people best qualified to tell me about the Bemba past. But what value could I attach to their stories? Fortunately with the Bemba there was, as it were, a built-in means of checking the reliability of what I was told. The Bemba have an extensive system of chieftainships, culminating in that of a paramount chief. The histories of these different chieftainships overlap and intertwine, and they also link up with the histories of the surrounding peoples, such as the Bisa, Lungu or Tabwa. I found that by collecting many of these histories it was possible to piece together a fairly consistent and coherent account of Bemba political history for at least the century or so before British rule began in 1899. By comparing a number of testimonies, describing the same events from different points of view, I was usually able to see what was most likely to have happened. Uncertainty about details and motives might well remain, but this can be true of even the best-documented history. And besides the checking of local traditions against each other, I was also able, here and there, to check them against the records of early travellers, which also provide dates for some events.

There is, however, one major weakness in Bemba traditions —a weakness common to many oral traditions. It is above all the chiefs who make and preserve history. Unlike some other societies in Africa, the Bemba are divided by no sharp distinctions of physical type, culture or mode of economy, such as might give ordinary people a special interest in preserving history independently of their rulers. By and large, Bemba commoners accept the history of their chiefs as being their own history. This point is of special importance when we look into the beginnings of Bemba history.

The Bemba account for their origins with a story which tells how their first chiefs were expelled from some kingdom far to the west, in a country called Luba. After many adventures, they settled in their present country, killing or driving out the earlier inhabitants. This story, like other legends of tribal origin, is decorated with many fanciful and miraculous episodes. Rather than accept it uncritically as the chronicle of a whole tribe on the march, we should see the Bemba story of migration as a vivid and memorable explanation of how the main features of Bemba chieftainship came into being. Bearing this in mind, and comparing other similar traditions in the region, we may suggest a more probable, if less dramatic, version of Bemba origins.

From some time before the sixteenth century, shifting cultivators, similar in culture to the Bemba of today, may have been moving into what is now eastern Zambia from the Congo basin, to the west and north-west. These peoples, unlike the Plateau Tonga farther south, were organized in chiefdoms, albeit small ones. At a late stage in these migrations, in the seventeenth century, there arrived a group of the Crocodile clan, probably from one of the Luba states bordering the Lunda empire of Mwata Yamvo in what is now western Katanga. These migrants settled in the middle of the great plateau to the south of Lake Tanganyika. Here they subdued and replaced the earlier chiefs, but they took over some of the customs of their subjects, and together with them formed the tribe since known as the Bemba.

The next hundred years or so of Bemba history—up to about 1800—are not well remembered in tradition. It seems that the invading Crocodile clan established a number of chieftainships which were more or less autonomous and reserved to distinct lineages within the royal clan. They all, however, recognized their paramount, Chitimukulu, as a kind of 'Divine king' with certain overriding ritual powers over the land. On the death of one Chitimukulu, chiefly lineages competed to obtain the paramountcy for one of their own members: there were frequent succession wars.

Around 1800 Bemba history took a new turn. It seems that

two successive Chitimukulus from the same lineage were able to take advantage of recent minor conquests to build up the power of their own lineage as against those of their rivals. Two new chieftainships were established: one, which was later called Mwamba, was given to the brother of a reigning Chitimukulu, and another to the son of his successor. This last appointment was a striking innovation, for Bemba chiefs, like Bemba commoners, trace descent in the female line; succession passes from brother to brother and then to their sisters' sons. By delegating power to their own sons, who were ineligible for the top posts, Bemba paramounts acquired subordinates whom they had no need to fear as rivals. And territory that was under the control of their own close relatives, whether brothers, sons or nephews, was more amenable to their personal influence than the territory of chiefs who were only very distantly related to the ruling lineage and who were accustomed to deciding most issues for themselves.

These innovations set the pattern for Bemba history throughout most of the nineteenth century. Conquest and centralization are the main themes of this period. Having consolidated its hold on the paramountcy, the dominant lineage proceeded to increase its power at the expense of the other chiefly lineages. It did this in two ways. First, it continued the trend of assigning newly conquered territory to close relatives of the paramount. Second, it made use of opportunities to place its own members in chieftainships which had formerly been held by other lineages.

We have a vivid witness to Bemba conquests in the journal kept by the Portuguese explorer Antonio Gamitto, who in 1831 and 1832 travelled north-west from Mozambique along an African trade route into the interior. This route passed through country which the Bemba had lately taken from their southern neighbours, the Bisa. Gamitto was told that the Bemba sought access to the cloth and other imports which the Bisa obtained from the Portuguese in exchange for ivory and copper. The Bemba seem to have failed in this attempt, for the Bisa continued to handle this trade, as Livingstone found in the 1860s. But the Bisa chiefs were unable to put up more than occasional resistance against the more highly organized Bemba, and in any case the Bemba soon had access to another trade route. This lay to the north, and was operated by Arabs and Swahili, who were mostly based on the Sultanate of Zanzibar. By 1850, Zanzibar had to meet a rising European demand for ivory, and the powerful Bemba chiefs were willing and useful agents in the profitable, if wasteful, business of hunting elephant—and not only elephant but also slaves. In return, Bemba chiefs obtained guns, cloth and beads. With these they armed and rewarded their followers and obtained further support for fresh raids and conquests.

In one way, Bemba expansion had the effect of integrating the Bemba political system. It made room for the creation of many new chieftainships, all held by more or less close relatives of Chitimukulu, the paramount. Those who were his brothers or nephews were knit together by the opportunities for promotion, according to genealogical seniority, from one chieftainship to another, up to the paramountcy itself. In the long run, however, expansion aggravated the tendencies to division and secession within the system. There was no standing army or centralized corps of administrators, and Chitimukulu never managed to gain a monopoly over the long-distance trade. Border chiefs, well placed for extending the range of ivory and slave hunts, valued their trade more highly than their chances of promotion to senior, but less profitable posts. And the Mwamba chieftainship, itself of fairly recent foundation, built up a sphere of influence which rivalled that of Chitimukulu. In 1883 a Chitimukulu and a Mwamba both died, and there were several new appointments and promotions throughout the Bemba hierarchy. The effect of these was to bring to the surface rivalries already inherent in Bemba geography and genealogy.

At this very period of internal crisis, the Bemba faced the

most serious external threat of their history. They had managed, after a series of battles, to beat off the Ngoni war-bands who had come north from Natal and for a time roamed the north-eastern plateau of Zambia. But the Bemba now had to deal with a growing number of Europeans—missionaries, traders and government officials—who occupied the country north and east of the Bemba in the last years of the nineteenth century. The Europeans, who increasingly obstructed the path of Bemba raiding and trading, feared they would have to fight it out with this warlike tribe. But the Bemba had no concerted anti-white policy. Prudently, they refrained from attacking Europeans, and the attitudes of the more important chiefs to these intruders were shaped by the shifting pattern of rivalries and alliances among the Bemba themselves. For a while, Bemba chiefs put out feelers towards the Europeans, assessing their strength and usefulness in comparison with that of the Arab and Swahili traders. From 1896, Chitimukulu was quite overshadowed by Mwamba. Mwamba died in 1898, and officials of Rhodes's British South Africa Company brought the Bemba under British rule after no more than a few skirmishes with minor border chiefs.

This pliant submission of the formidable Bemba revealed weaknesses in their political system; yet these had their advantages. They averted the need for a head-on collision with superior force. Elsewhere in Africa, such collisions sometimes led to the break-up of tribal organizations. The Bemba, however, not only escaped the stigma of defeat, they preserved their traditional political structure into the twentieth century.

CHAPTER ELEVEN

Early Farmers and Traders North of the Zambezi

Brian M. Fagan

OVER THE PAST TEN YEARS archaeological discoveries in Zambia have provided new information about the people who lived in the area since the beginning of the Iron Age some two thousand years ago. Thanks to the new radiocarbon methods, we have been able to date even the humble village settlements of ordinary people, and to watch their progress from the time when they first began to use iron for their tools and weapons, until the time, some 1,500 years later, when written documents and oral traditions provide evidence for more detailed history.

The more recent history of the country which we know today as Zambia is comparatively well known. Zambia lies immediately to the north of the middle part of the Zambezi River. Most of it is a high-altitude plateau covered with monotonous tracts of savannah woodland, relieved by the deep river valleys of the Zambezi and its northern tributaries, the Kafue and the Luangwa. Where eastern Zambia juts up northwards its boundary with the Congo follows the course of the valley of the Luapula River. The presence of this valley has always made it easy for people from the Congo basin to cross into northern Zambia. During the past five hundred years Zambia has been settled by many conquering groups from the Congo who moved southwards and eastwards across the Luapula. The history of the little states resulting

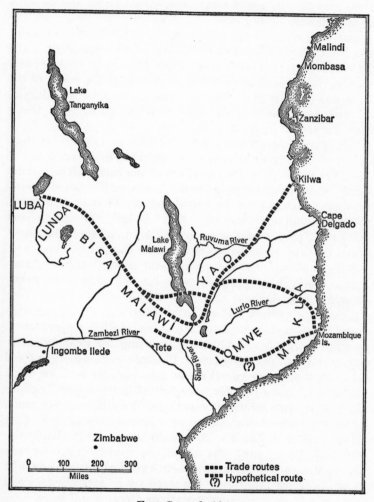

East Central Africa

from these conquests is known from oral histories which have been recorded by many historians, missionaries and government officers.

But until recently our knowledge of older Zambian history has been scanty. For most of the last two thousand years the Zambian plateau was remote from the great trade routes which criss-crossed the Rhodesian plateau to the south of the Zambezi. In that area the trade routes brought wealth, and the rich stone-built capital sites of Rhodesia suggest also a high degree of political organization.

But Zambia presents a different picture. There the only evidence that exists of long-distance trade is confined to the Zambezi valley. The iron-workers of the savannah woodland north of the river were isolated from anything but the most sporadic contacts with the outside world. They lived in small scattered communities and they lacked the centralized chieftainships and elaborate organization which were introduced by the later conquerors from the Congo.

This much we have known for some time. But the archaeological work of the past ten years has helped us to fill in the picture a good deal.

By chance, pottery and a possible fragment of iron ore were found on an ancient land surface at the Machili forest station in western Zambia. Archaeologists using the modern radiocarbon methods of dating (see J. R. Gray, page 42) have fixed the date of these as round about A.D. 100. So we now think that iron-working peoples were settled in the upper Zambezi basin nearly two thousand years ago. We still have not much information about these earliest iron-workers or how they came to settle in Zambia. But we do know that gradually the whole of the country was settled by iron-working farmers who ousted or absorbed the Stone Age Bushmen people who lived thinly scattered over the territory in rock shelters and caves and in open encampments near streams and lakes.

Iron Age people were widely settled over the Zambian plateau by the seventh century A.D., some of them the direct descendants of the earliest settlers, while others were more recent immigrants. A comparatively dense population of early Iron Age farmers lived on the Batoka plateau in southern Zambia. They are known as the Kalomo people, and their settlements extend from the borders of Barotseland in the west to the Middle Zambezi in the east. Today most of the villages appear as small mounds averaging two hundred yards in length and ten feet in height. They are concentrated on the high-altitude grasslands of the Batoka plateau. Two of these villages have been carefully excavated and radiocarbon dates have shown that they were occupied from as early as the seventh century until the thirteenth century A.D.

The inhabitants were cultivating sorghum, perhaps millet, and a variety of minor crops, including beans. They had herds of shorthorn cattle, sheep and goats and many chickens and dogs. For much of their meat supply the earliest Kalomo people relied on hunting and scavenging. Wild roots and fruits and vegetables were gathered for the pot. Simple pottery was made with grooved decoration in the earlier stages, and later on with economically designed, stamped and incised motifs. Some of these pots are similar to vessels of the same period from early Rhodesian villages, which shows that many communities of the same general character were inhabiting southern Africa at this time.

Iron hoes and weighted digging-sticks were used for cultivating. Only the simplest of methods can have been employed and this would have meant careful soil selection, because the iron implements would have been quite inadequate for large-scale bush clearance. The soil scientists who analysed the deposits of the Kalomo mounds have shown that the traditional village sites were abandoned at regular intervals, presumably when the plots around them were exhausted. Probably the inhabitants moved their possessions to nearby traditional sites on a regular rotation basis over successive generations.

The largest of the Kalomo mounds, Isamu Pati, was

excavated on a sufficient scale for us to be able to reconstruct the appearance of the village in its later stages. On the flat top of the village there were pole and mud huts, as well as grain bins, built around a central enclosure. The whole village must have been protected from wild animals and raiders by a thorn fence, for no traces of post holes or a stockade were found. Soil analysis has shown that the phosphate content of the deposits of the central enclosure is much higher than that of the rest of the village, which may mean that it was used as a cattle kraal.

Nine skeletons lay in shallow graves in the enclosure. The bodies were tightly contracted, with the knees at the chin, and they were almost devoid of any personal ornament. In one case the body of a young girl, which lay near the remains of a hut, was found buried with two sea-shells and many glass and shell beads. The skeletons show that the people were of a mixed Negro and Bush physical type.

These Kalomo communities formed little isolated groups of mixed farming peoples, whose simple material culture and rudimentary social organization was typical of many Iron Age groups in southern Africa a thousand years ago. One of the most striking features of the Kalomo villages and other early settlements of iron-workers is the scarcity of objects imported from the outside world such as glass beads. Only twenty-eight glass beads were found in all the deposits at Isamu Pati, an eloquent testimony to the isolation of many of the early Iron Age communities.

Down in the Zambezi valley itself a very different picture emerges. The Zambezi pours out of the Batoka gorges, sixty miles downstream from the Victoria Falls. Then it flows placidly through a flat-bottomed valley often called the Gwembe. This hot, inhospitable valley was the home of enormous herds of elephants, whose tusks were a valuable asset to the people of the Gwembe. And this meant contact with the outside world. For more than fifteen hundred years the east coast of Africa was visited by merchants from Asia in search of precious metals and especially of ivory. The tusks of the African elephant are particularly suitable for making the ivory bracelets and other ornaments much favoured in the East. So there was a constant and insatiable demand for African ivory, which stimulated a brisk trade in tusks in the far interior. Gold, copper, iron and other raw materials were also handled and bartered for exotic imports such as sea-shells, glass beads, cloth and porcelain vessels.

Isolated finds of glass beads and sea-shells are known from the remains of early Iron Age villages in Rhodesia dating from as early as the second century A.D. We know little of this early trade. But the Ingombe Ilede settlement, recently discovered on the Zambian side of the Middle Zambezi, has added much to our knowledge of the early history of the ivory trade.

Ingombe Ilede was discovered by accident during the construction of a water-pumping station in 1960. The settlement lies on the summit of a low hill near the confluence of the Lusitu stream with the Zambezi some thirty-two miles downstream from Kariba.

The occupation levels of the site are eight feet deep, and have been radiocarbon dated to between the seventh and tenth centuries A.D. In its earliest phase, the Ingombe Ilede settlement appears to have been occupied by a group of elephant hunters. Perhaps they were from the Batoka plateau, for their pottery bears some resemblance to that of early peoples from the northern part of the highlands.

Like their neighbours on the Batoka plateau, Ingombe Ilede people were cultivating sorghum, and probably millet. They kept cows, goats, chickens and dogs as well as gathering wild vegetable foods for the pot. Many small antelopes were hunted and edible rodents were trapped and eaten. In many respects their life seems to have been similar to that of the Tonga farmers who live in the area today.

The people lived in flimsy huts made, as far as we can tell, from perishable materials such as wood and grass. They

buried their dead in the village and at the edges of the settlement, while their tools and weapons were of the simplest
designs.

In the earlier levels that have been excavated imported
objects, such as glass beads, are rare. But when we come to the
later stages of the development of Ingombe Ilede, imported
goods are more common and we find that the inhabitants were
making fine bowls and beakers quite unlike the cruder early
pots. Here is yet another indication of developing contacts
with the outside world.

Further such evidence emerged when the archaeologists
found the graves of the most important inhabitants of Ingombe
Ilede. These were all buried in the centre of the site and they
wore strings of gold, glass and shell beads at the neck and
waist. Their limbs were encased in copper bangles and the
metal had preserved fragments of cotton and bark-cloth gar-
ments which they had worn. Specialists have shown that
some of the cloth was imported, the remainder probably
woven on the Zambezi. Copper ingots, trade wire and iron
implements for making bangle wire lay by the head and feet
of several skeletons, together with imported ceremonial
hoes and gongs. Other bodies were buried with quantities of
pottery or sea-shells. All these rich grave-goods point to their
owners having been engaged in trading activities.

Ingombe Ilede is sited in a strategic position. The village
is in an elephant-infested area. And what is more there are
easy routes from the village to the nearest gold and copper
workings on the plateau. Some mines are as little as one
hundred and fifty miles away. Another asset was the nearby
salt-workings. When David Livingstone passed through the
valley in 1860, the Lusitu stream was the scene of great salt-
working activity. Salt was an immensely valuable commodity
in early Africa and a vital element of domestic trade. Undoubtedly the Ingombe Ilede people made use of it to
strengthen their position as middlemen between the Zambezi
traders and the miners of the plateau.

The trade must have been sporadic and for most of the time the Ingombe Ilede people lived the life of subsistence farmers. Archaeological evidence also shows that the trade was in the hands of a few individuals, for skeletons in graves outside the central site, favoured by the most important inhabitants, bear little or no personal adornment.

We are still uncertain of the wider historical role of Ingombe Ilede. Chronologically it belongs to the period immediately before the emergence of states on the Rhodesian plateau to the south. And we do know that the settlement was an important centre for the Zambezi trade in the centuries before the great expansion of the Rhodesian gold trade about a thousand years ago. As far as we can establish, the decline of Ingombe Ilede seems to have started at the time when the stone builders of the south began seriously to develop their commerce.

The significance of the recent Zambian discoveries lies in the light they have thrown on the economic patterns of early iron-working peoples at a period remote from oral or written records. Kalomo communities were typical of many early Iron Age farming groups in southern Africa a thousand years ago. And the discoveries at Ingombe Ilede show that even at this early time the outside world was conscious of the Zambezi's economic possibilities.

CHAPTER TWELVE

North of the Zambezi

E. A. Alpers

SOME YEARS AGO in a broadcast talk, Professor Roland Oliver said of the Portuguese that 'north of the Zambezi they were entirely ignorant of the interior'. Considering the state of research in the late 1950s his conclusion was inescapable. But since then a further body of most valuable Portuguese documents has come to light. Today we still accept that the Portuguese were mainly preoccupied with the area south of the Zambezi. But the new evidence shows that they were by no means totally ignorant of the interior to the north. Indeed, work on these Portuguese documents has given us important new information about the area north of the Zambezi. In particular we have been able to add to our knowledge of long-distance trading in the region.

This area, which is more conveniently called east central Africa, is characterized by lightly wooded grasslands, punctuated by several considerable ranges of hills. These ranges run mainly from north to south, and though they are by no means impassable, the easiest and oldest lines of communication follow the lines between them. The region is very nearly divided in half by Lake Malawi and the Shire River, which flows south from the lake to the Zambezi. Before the population movements of the nineteenth century, the area round the south of Lake Malawi and the Shire River was inhabited by the Malawi people. To the west of the Malawi lived the Bisa. To the east of the Malawi lived the Yao, the Lomwe and the Makua Lomwe peoples. All of these people speak closely

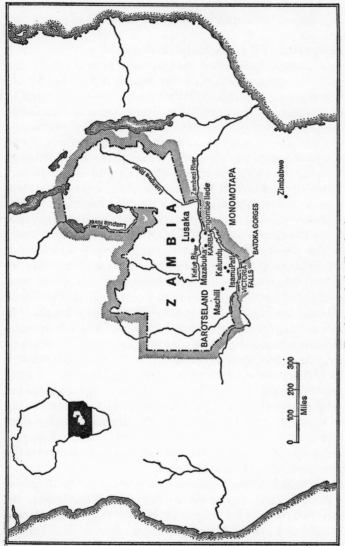

Zambia and the Zambezi

related Bantu languages and share a common pattern of social and political organization based on the principle of matrilineal descent.

East central Africa was, and indeed still is, a region rich in ivory. There are indications that, at least as early as the end of the first millennium A.D., ivory was being traded southwards down to the Zambezi, the natural route to the interior, where Arab and Swahili merchants purchased it at established market towns. From there they carried it downstream to the sea and then northwards again to the developing Swahili city states which dotted the coast above the mouth of the Ruvuma River in the north-east of this region. From these the ivory was generally exported to India, where there was a constant demand for the soft, easily worked ivory of Africa. It is clear from archaeological excavations undertaken at Ingombe Ilede, on the north bank of the Zambezi, some thirty miles below the Kariba Gorge, that Katanga copper was also an important item of trade in east central Africa. (See Brian M. Fagan's article, page 76.) Nevertheless, all this trade from north of the Zambezi was secondary to that from the south, which was based on gold from the Rhodesian plateau area. When the Portuguese arrived in East Africa at the beginning of the sixteenth century, they concentrated all their efforts on securing this gold trade for themselves. Failing to control it from the coast, they began to move up the Zambezi as early as 1530 in order to achieve their aim. By seizing control of the Zambezi route, the Portuguese deprived the Africans living to the north of the river of the traditional markets for their ivory and copper. For, unlike their Arab and Swahili predecessors up the Zambezi, the Portuguese had no interest in the commerce of east central Africa.

The principal African traders to the north of the Zambezi were the Malawi. According to their court traditions, the Malawi had originally migrated to the region south and south-west of Lake Malawi from Luba country, in Katanga. We realize, however, that this was not the migration of an entire nation, but rather that of a relatively limited number of invaders who imposed their rule on the people whom they found there. While there is no direct archaeological evidence for dating their arrival in east central Africa, there are indications that the Malawi rulers were part of a general migration from the Congo, which occurred perhaps in the late thirteenth century. Indeed, there are Malawi chiefly clans in Rhodesia whose traditions and genealogies show that they arrived south of the Zambezi early in the fourteenth century. This dating probably applies equally to the greater part of the Malawi invaders who remained north of the river.

It is my belief that, when the Portuguese moved up the Zambezi, the Malawi chiefs had a considerable economic stake in the ivory and copper trade to Swahili and Arab merchants along the river. If this was so, the Portuguese action appears to have deprived them of that market without replacing it with an alternative outlet for their goods. It may well be that the resultant economic pressure was at the root of the dissensions which threatened to topple the established hierarchy of the Malawi state, which had been based on conquest and was probably cemented by royal control of trade. Court traditions have little to say on this subject, but this is only to be expected; for the function of these traditions is to preserve and to justify the existing power structure. Portuguese sources, however, reveal very clearly that such a crisis existed by the last quarter of the sixteenth century.

This crisis was apparently the culmination of political and economic rivalry between the Malawi paramount chief, who was entitled Kalonga, and his lieutenant on the Shire River, who was known as Lundu. The conflict led Lundu to seek to create an independent kingdom of his own, beyond the limits of the Kalonga's influence. In the late 1580s Lundu's followers invaded the south-eastern part of northern Mozambique and established what the Portuguese came to call the kingdom of Bororo. This invasion is clearly documented not only by

81

contemporary Portuguese observers, but also by oral traditions collected in that area at the beginning of the present century by the Portuguese official, Eduardo do Couto Lupi.

Years of turbulence followed this extension of Malawi influence. It was probably not until the second decade of the seventeenth century that order was restored in east central Africa, when the Kalonga Musura, aided by the Portuguese, defeated Lundu and re-established his paramountcy throughout Malawi-dominated country, including Bororo.

The keystone of this Malawi empire was trade. While the Kalonga was widely recognized as paramount chief, there was apparently neither a centralized civil administration nor a unified military control. The Kalonga's capital was near the south-west corner of Lake Malawi and he ruled the surrounding area. Outside this area each great Malawi sectional chief, including even Lundu, was left to rule his own district. It seems that the only effective cohesive element in this empire was Malawi domination of long-distance trade. By the 1630s the Malawi were trading along a well-established route through Makua and Lomwe country to the mainland opposite Mozambique Island. There the locally settled Portuguese inhabitants actively cultivated the overland ivory trade with the Malawi. Portuguese records show that the development of this trade route resulted from the extension of Malawi influence over Bororo. We may therefore suggest that the genesis of this important new trade route is to be found in the Malawi reaction to the arrival of the Portuguese in east central Africa.

One other great long-distance trade route developed in this region. It ran from Malawi country north-east to Kilwa, on the coast of southern Tanzania. It appears that two separate factors combined to create this route during the second half of the sixteenth century. Although it had been a great trading centre in medieval times, Kilwa's prosperity was based exclusively on its seaborne trade to the south. Kilwa, situated on an island, naturally looked to the sea and had only minimal commercial ties with the immediate interior. As with the Malawi, it was the Portuguese intrusion which forced Kilwa to seek a new source of trade. By severely limiting Kilwa's seaborne trade with the Zambezi and Rhodesian gold area, the Portuguese turned the attention of its Swahili merchants inward, towards the Tanzanian hinterland. Thus, at the coast, the Kilwa route owed its origin to African reaction to outside influence.

Nevertheless, it was not the Swahili who penetrated inland, but the Africans of the interior who travelled to Kilwa. The impetus for trading with the coast came from the Yao, in north-west Mozambique, rather than from the coast. The rise of the Yao as great long-distance traders does not, however, appear necessarily to have been a reaction to the arrival of the Portuguese. We cannot rule out this possibility, but a reading of the only published collection of Yao tradition, compiled by an Anglican priest who was himself a Yao, suggests that it was the internal dynamics of Yao society which caused them to forge a route to Kilwa. On this crucial point Portuguese sources do, in fact, appear to be quite silent, for the Portuguese had almost no direct contact with Yaoland until the late nineteenth century. We must hope that the solution to this problem may yet emerge from the oral traditions of the Yao, when these have been more fully recorded.

In any case, we know that by 1616, when Gaspar Bocarro travelled overland from Tete on the Zambezi to Kilwa, this route was well established. By the end of the seventeenth century, the Yao had also replaced the Malawi as the dominant traders to Mozambique Island. This was probably due to a combination of factors, including the increasing political disintegration of the Malawi empire, the commercial aggressiveness of the Yao, and the assertion of Makua-Lomwe independence from Malawi commercial influence, which would have led to the disruption of the Malawi trade route through Bororo to Mozambique Island. Furthermore, Malawi influence continued to decline during the eighteenth century, as the various sections of the Malawi nation continued to grow apart.

Despite this and other changes, the basic pattern of long-distance trade in east central Africa, which was established during the century following Portuguese penetration up the Zambezi, remained essentially unaltered for more than two centuries. One should note, however, that the substance of trade began to change gradually from the middle of the eighteenth century, as the presence of both French and Brazilian slavers at Mozambique Island, and of the Omani Arabs at Kilwa, created a new demand for slaves. By the early decades of the nineteenth century, slaves were challenging ivory as the staple item of trade in east central Africa.

The pattern of trade in the region was seriously altered by the Ngoni invasions from southern Africa in the mid-nineteenth century. The Ngoni, a warlike people who are related to the Zulu, dislocated many societies throughout the area, in particular the Malawi peoples, thereby creating a ready supply for the increasingly voracious Kilwa slave market. At the same time, the Yao were attacked from the east by both the Makua and the Lomwe. Far from weakening their influence, the resultant dispersal of Yao sections into southern Malawi and southern Tanzania actually strengthened it, for the Yao now entered these areas as conquering invaders, and not as peaceful traders. The collapse of the earlier commerical network exposed east central Africa to increasing social and political chaos, but it also led to the establishment of a new political order. In many respects it marks the beginning of the modern period in this part of Africa.

CHAPTER THIRTEEN

The Rise of the Zulu Kingdom

Shula Marks

'A WONDERFUL PEOPLE THE ZULUS', Benjamin Disraeli is said to have commented in 1879. 'They beat our generals, they convert our bishops and they write "finis" to a French dynasty.' The Zulu were indeed a remarkable people, but perhaps it was for other reasons than those suggested by Disraeli.

At the beginning of the nineteenth century the Zulu were one of the numerous small chiefdoms of Bantu-speaking Nguni people who lived along the south-east coast of Africa, from Delagoa Bay in the north to the Great Fish River in the south. Within little more than a decade they had conquered and absorbed most of the peoples in the neighbourhood of present-day Zululand, devastated Natal to the south, and set in motion a mighty snowball of tribal movement and conquest. As a result of their rise, tribe was sent reeling against tribe and the interior plateau of southern Africa became a chaotic mass of people on the move. To this day the whole era is called by the Nguni and Sotho peoples of South Africa the *Mfecane*—The Crushing. Nor were the effects limited to southern Africa. Tribes and fragments of tribes ricocheted off as far away as Tanzania and Malawi to the north-east and Barotseland in modern Zambia to the north-west. For the peoples of eastern and central Africa their advent was amongst the most significant and dramatic events in their nineteenth-century history.

Why then, and how, did this explosion occur? At the time

—and indeed until quite recently—it was customary to see Shaka, the man who became chief of the Zulu people in 1816, as the key figure behind the entire *Mfecane*.

Shaka was undoubtedly a military genius who revolutionized Nguni warfare. He may well have been a cruel tyrant who waged war for war's sake. But even so it is unlikely that he was the 'Scourge of God' solely responsible for the great upheaval I have described. Recent research suggests that behind Shaka, behind the *Mfecane*, lay the pressures of population explosion and soil exhaustion.

Clan histories and the genealogies of Bantu-speaking people all over southern Africa suggest that there was a rapid population growth from about the end of the seventeenth century. The northern Nguni area of Natal-Zululand could have had special reasons for an unusually swift rise in population. This region, which I shall call northern Nguniland from now on, occupies the lowland belt between the Indian Ocean coast on the east and the high plateau of the Transvaal to the west. It is the area of highest rainfall in southern Africa. Its soil is fertile, its vegetation lush and semi-tropical. The climate, except at the extreme north, is temperate and healthy to man and beast.

From perhaps as early as the thirteenth century Bantu-speaking peoples had been drifting into this area. It was ideally suited to their needs as mixed farmers, who grew grain and other vegetables, but who prided themselves above all on their herds of sleek short-horned cattle. It looks as if ripples of movement into this naturally attractive area may have continued into the eighteenth century. Already by the beginning of that century some tribes had spilt over from the coastlands into the less inviting interior.

It is also very possible that the natural rate of population increase in northern Nguniland was further accelerated by the introduction of maize as a new and highly efficient food-crop. There is some argument about the exact date of the introduction of maize, but it seems probable that it was first introduced into southern Africa through northern Nguniland, and that it came through the Tembe Thonga people living on its boundaries in Portuguese East Africa. The significance of maize as a high-yielding, disease-resisting crop in areas of high rainfall is that it cuts down famine and so eliminates the periodic reduction of population through famine which is experienced by most communities which are purely agrarian.

However, even in such a very hospitable area the soil can only support a limited number of pastoralists like the Nguni, who practise shifting cultivation. It may well be that with the rise in population the effects of soil exhaustion were in some areas already being felt by the beginning of the nineteenth century. The disastrous famine of 1802, remembered in tradition, could have been a symptom of this. It could also have been a major spur to militant action. Tribes faced with want and depression began to rub up against their neighbours and to look longingly at their land and cattle.

On the one hand the rapid growth of population can lead to uncoordinated aggression. On the other hand it may act as a stimulus to deal with the problems of frustration and aggression in a rational way. It can bring about a more co-ordinated form of social organization if far-sighted political leaders create large confederacies out of squabbling chiefdoms. Some time before the advent of Shaka this seems to have been happening in northern Nguniland. By the beginning of the nineteenth century there were at least four or five larger chiefdoms which were beginning to dominate and absorb their neighbours: the Ndwandwe, the Mtetwa, the Hlubi and the Ngwane. Later, the Ndwandwe confederacy was to prove the most formidable rival of the Zulu. Once defeated by Shaka they were to become the progenitors of the Ngoni kingdoms of eastern and central Africa, and the Gaza kingdom of Mozambique. The Hlubi and Ngwane peoples were to precipitate much of the turmoil of the interior of southern Africa, while one group of the Ngwane people were to form the Swazi nation. At the beginning of the nineteenth century, under Shaka's father, the Zulu were simply one of many tributaries of the Mtetwa confederacy which was ruled by a great chief called Dingiswayo. Shaka himself served as one of Dingiswayo's military commanders.

How then was this puny and subordinate Zulu chiefdom, occupying a territory no larger than the smallest English county, able to set these larger confederacies in motion, to expand its control over an area larger than Europe? How was it able to stamp its character and culture—indeed its name— on all the surrounding peoples of Natal-Zululand? The main answer seems to lie in the new military techniques, introduced by the Mtetwa chief, Dingiswayo, but revolutionized by Shaka. Here it should be added that it is not always possible to distinguish between those reforms introduced by Dingiswayo and those introduced by Shaka. Tribal tradition, on which we are largely dependent, tends to blur the two. Nevertheless it is likely that Dingiswayo introduced the profound change of organizing men for war in age-set regiments, while Shaka was responsible for the drill of these regiments and the strategic formation resembling the horns of a buffalo, in which they advanced to envelop the enemy. Shaka also replaced the old throwing assegai with his new short, and far more deadly, stabbing spear. Another of his innovations was his concept of total war. He was a master of strategy and psychological warfare.

Dingiswayo's military regiments were composed of men of the same age, recruited from all the villages of the kingdom and all its separate clans, on their attaining adulthood. They were stationed at specially erected royal barracks, and owed their loyalty to the king alone. The formation of these regiments, with their firm loyalty to a central authority, helped to unify and consolidate the kingdom. Through them too all men of military age could be trained and drilled in a way no other Nguni army had been before. Each regiment was divided into companies and each individual in each company was drilled to know his exact place in the strategy of the whole. It was the perfect drill, discipline and speed of the Zulu which in 1879 was to inflict disaster even on a British army.

During colonial times, the evolution of this new type of warfare was attributed to external influence. The tradition that Dingiswayo, while in exile from his own people, had met a white man and had returned to his tribe riding a horse and carrying a gun was given the widest interpretation. From this solitary white man Dingiswayo was supposed to have gathered all his innovating ideas. Even supposing that he did meet a white or half-caste traveller, it seems unlikely that such a man should have spoken a language intelligible to Dingiswayo and virtually incredible that he conveyed to him all the intricacies of European military methods.

In fact, it may not be necessary to look for external influences in the evolution of the Zulu army. It can be argued that in a period of continual skirmishing, which reached its crescendo under Shaka, it would be natural for new methods of more intensive fighting to evolve. The regimental system was a logical conversion for military purposes of traditional circumcision lodges and might well have occurred to someone who had seen the rudimentary age-regiment system practised by the Sotho people. Dingiswayo had probably met these in the course of his travels.

While the Sotho age-regiments may have been the basis for Dingiswayo's military regiments, their example does not, however, provide an adequate explanation for the very new ideas of dividing regiments into companies, their drill and strategic formation. It was these aspects of the Zulu army, taken together with its new weapon, which gave it its very remarkable striking power, and for these things some further explanation appears to be necessary.

We know that in the first year of his reign Dingiswayo sent a hundred head of cattle and ivory tusks to the Portuguese settlement at Delagoa Bay in the hope of opening up direct trade. At the same time he asked Makasana, chief of the

Tembe Thonga people, who lived just south of the Bay, to send him soldiers to help him oust a rival brother. Now the Tembe Thonga were the main intermediaries of the trade between the Portuguese and the northern Nguni. Is it not possible that they were also pedlars of ideas, who brought some notion of European drill and military formation to the northern Nguni? As yet we know far too little of the history of the peoples of south Mozambique in the eighteenth and early nineteenth century to give final answers to these questions. Yet it is surely not without significance that the first Portuguese settlement of any permanence at Delagoa Bay was made in 1787. Nine years later the eighty men of the garrison there were forced to take refuge in the bush for a year. It may therefore be that the genius of the Mtetwa chief or his Zulu commander lay in his grasp of the significance of Portuguese military methods transmitted through the Tembe Thonga and in their brilliant adaptation of European stylized warfare to Nguni social organization. Nguni society was ready and adapted for the change—it needed but a single spark to set it in motion. Other tribes were quick to follow the reforms adopted by Shaka and Dingiswayo and to use them in turn to their own advantage against the unprepared people of the interior.

It was the destructive aspects of the *Mfecane* which were most immediately felt. The social disorder and disintegration are not hard to imagine and the effects of marauding tribes on the move are easy to catalogue. For many the choice was to join the invaders or set off themselves in search of a fresh victim. Refugees scrambled to safety in broken, barren, hilly country. Some even turned to cannibalism in their desperation. Yet the *Mfecane* was far from being solely a negative and senseless era of murder, pillage and destruction. For out of this maelstrom new peoples, even new nations, were born. The demography of southern, central and eastern Africa, as well as their political and social configuration, were profoundly altered. Shaka's achievement in welding a multi-tribal nation out of the numerous tribes of Nguniland in the short span of twelve years, a nation which has long outlasted the military power on which its greatness was based, was in itself outstanding. Consider, next, the achievements of those leaders who broke away on nation-building exploits of their own. Consider Mziligazi, who started off with some three hundred followers and created the entirely new state of the Ndebele, or Matabele, of Rhodesia out of people of the most diverse ethnic origins. Consider Zwegendaba, who carried his followers over two thousand miles from their homeland. To this day his people have retained their character and social organization in Malawi and Tanzania despite the long period of absorption of non-Nguni elements and their splintering into several Ngoni kingdoms.

And the positive effects were not limited to those people who were direct offshoots from Nguniland. For those who were not crushed by their advent, the invaders brought a challenge and an example of military and social organization. Thus the Basuto nation was literally created at this time by their astute diplomat-king, Moshesh. And farther north, in the Transvaal, Zambia and Tanzania, previously disorganized people were also to profit from the Nguni example. It is frequently asserted that the Shakan wars paved the way for European expansion in southern Africa, just as the Ngoni invasions in eastern Africa profited the Arab slaver. In part this may be true. Yet in both cases it can also be argued that the *Mfecane* had in addition a positive effect. It was often those people who were either Nguni offshoots, or who had responded positively to the Nguni challenge, who were able to withstand the vicissitudes of the nineteenth century and to resist newer invaders—whether Voortrekkers, Arab slave traders or even the colonial regimes at the turn of the century.

CHAPTER FOURTEEN

The Middle Age of African History

Roland Oliver

DURING THE YEARS since the first series of talks was broadcast under the title *The Dawn of African History*, African history has established itself, not only in Africa, but almost all over the world. At all the English-speaking universities in tropical Africa a history degree means first and foremost a degree in the history of Africa, and the history graduates of these universities, numbering by now many hundreds, are carrying the message out into the secondary schools of all their countries. In French-speaking Africa the process is not so far advanced, but it is at least beginning. Outside Africa, in Europe and North America, there are now some three or four dozen universities in which African history is regularly taught. Research students, in training for university posts, are now enrolled from countries as remote from Africa as Canada and the West Indies, Israel, India and Japan. If we include those now in training, there must today be getting on for a thousand people around the world who are actively engaged in extending the frontiers of knowledge in one part or another of this subject. What, then, are all these people actually doing?

Two hundred of them, perhaps, are archaeologists and prehistorians. These are the people who search for and excavate sites occupied by men, since the time when our earliest human ancestors started to chip stones and fashion them into simple tools, somewhere between a million and two million years ago. Up till ten or fifteen years ago the emphasis in African archaeology was on the remote past, on the search for man's origins, and on the earliest stages of his progress as man. Today the emphasis is shifting to the more recent past, starting about ten thousand years ago, when man, after his infinitely slow development as a hunter and gatherer, was at last preparing himself to be a farmer, and so to till the earth and take charge of it in a way he had never done before. The emphasis from here on is no longer on man in general, but very definitely on man in Africa, and on his performance in the very varied kinds of African environment—the steppe, the light woodland, the forest, the mountain, the river valley, the lakeshore, the sea coast. The archaeologist of this period is not merely concerned with where farming originated, but with the stages by which it spread and developed, with the population growth to which it gave rise, with the question of how far these early farming communities of Africa laid out the basic pattern of linguistic and tribal divisions in the Africa of today. This means that archaeologists of this period must be regional specialists, and there must be many of them. Every university in Africa must have its complement. Every government in Africa must have its antiquities service. And, even so, every country in Africa will have room and to spare for visiting expeditions from overseas.

After the archaeologists come the historians proper. Where the archaeologist works from things, the historian works either from the written or the spoken word. The historian, therefore, is dependent at every stage on language, and the most meaningful way to analyse what historians are doing about African history today is to look at the languages through which they are working. Today—and this is perhaps the most striking contrast with the situation of nine years ago—there is a steadily growing nucleus of historians who are working wholly, or mainly, in the indigenous languages of Africa itself. Of the contributors to this series, Eike Haberland, Bethwell Ogot and Andrew Roberts are all people who have done their most important work in African languages.

Dr Ogot, if I may use him as an example, wrote a doctoral thesis for the University of London on the settlement of western Kenya and eastern Uganda by the Luo and Padhola peoples; it was based on three stout volumes of clan histories, collected mostly by himself in the course of interviewing living informants in these two areas. He first recorded the interviews on tape. He next transcribed them in the original languages. He then translated them into English, so that the whole community of African historians could use them and check his conclusions. This pattern of research is now being followed by many others. Naturally, this kind of work is most easily done by African scholars working in their own linguistic area, and the increasing availability of African research students has been an important stimulus to such inquiries. But non-African researchers, too, are showing an increasing readiness to work in African languages, as anthropologists have been doing for many years past, and to accept the long years of specialization in the languages and cultures of one local area which this involves. It is partly a matter of sheer numbers. When historians of Africa were few, they had to be jacks of all trades and masters of none. But as more people enter the field and knowledge grows, specialization becomes the order of the day. It is true that special difficulties face the historian in working from oral evidence, but these are no greater than the difficulties of working from many kinds of written evidence. Now that there is the willingness to specialize, the difficulties are being overcome.

Not all of the historians who are working in African languages are working on oral evidence. A few African languages have comparatively old written records. Ge'ez and Amharic, the two written languages of Ethiopia, have records surviving from medieval times, and a small but growing band of trained Ethiopian historians are now joining in the study of these documents. Swahili, Hausa and Malagasy all have written chronicles dating from before the colonial period, and these, too, are receiving attention from scholars. And, of course,

Arabic, though not in origin an African language, can be called one for this purpose, since it has been written and spoken in large areas of Africa from early medieval times onwards. The history of Egypt and North Africa has been studied mainly in Arabic sources since the coming of Islam. The new development has been the increasing discovery and use by historians of Arabic documents written in the parts of Africa south of the Sahara where Arabic has been the main language of religion and education. Arabic is an exceptionally difficult language to learn. It usually takes about five years for a beginner to acquire a reasonable fluency in handling historical manuscripts. Nevertheless, some people have learned it, and others are beginning to learn it, with a view to using it for the kind of African history described by Dr Levtzion in his talk in this series.

Some of the most significant progress of the past nine years has been made in the sources of African history written in the lesser-known European languages. For some two hundred years, from the mid-fifteenth century until the mid-seventeenth, the Europeans who sailed around the coasts of Africa and planted forts and small colonies on the beaches and off-shore islands were the Portuguese. And the missionaries who attempted the evangelization of Africa during the same period were all Roman Catholics, who wrote in Portuguese, Italian, Spanish or Latin. It is only in the last few years that these southern European archives have begun to be systematically searched by historians interested primarily in the history of Africa, and some of the fruits of this new work has been represented in this series by the contributions of Alan Ryder, David Birmingham, Walter Rodney and Edward Alpers. From the mid-seventeenth century onwards, the Portuguese were joined, not only by the British and the French, but also by the Dutch and the Danes. Here again the younger historians of Africa are hard at work, searching archives in The Hague and Copenhagen, Paris and London, as well as those in Lisbon and the Vatican. And it is important to realize that many of those who begin by working in the European archives of the pre-colonial period go on to work in the traditional history of African peoples. Their study of the written evidence of outside observers gives them a framework for further inquiry.

This series of contributions, like those published in *The Dawn of African History*, has been limited to the pre-colonial period of African history, because this is the period about which least is known. It would be quite misleading, however, to suppose that this is where most of the new historians of Africa are putting their main effort. Most of them, quite rightly, are working on the history of the past hundred years —quite rightly, because it is the past hundred years or so which most concern the living members of any society anywhere in the world. Here too, however, the last few years have seen a revolution in the methods and sources of history. The people who are studying the modern history of Africa today are doing so overwhelmingly in Africa. Most of what they are studying is written, and most of it is written in English or French. Much of it is indeed still written by non-African observers of the African scene. But no one nowadays is interested in studying the history of colonial policy by itself. They are concerned to see what happened to African peoples under colonial rule. They are not interested in what Governors wrote to London or Paris. They are interested in what District Commissioners wrote to Provincial Commissioners about the people in their Districts. They are interested, above all, in what Africans wrote both to Europeans and to each other. The questions they are most concerned to answer have to do with such things as the origins of nationalism, the significance of different kinds of resistance to colonial rule, the 'politics of survival' employed by the leaders of African societies and institutions under the pressures of alien influence. Very often this kind of work, too, involves working in African languages, and interviewing people as well as reading papers. In almost every case, how-

ever, it involves working in Africa; for one of the most surprising things that we have learned in the last few years is
that the vast preponderance of historical records for the
colonial period are to be found in Africa, and not in the
capitals of the countries which ruled Africa. It goes without
saying that the records of post-colonial Africa will similarly
be found within Africa and not outside.

What has been most surprising about the last decade has
been the speed with which the colonial period has receded
from the consciousness of independent Africa. The frontiers
of colonial Africa have remained so far intact, but within
them the new nations of Africa have been forced to carry out
great innovations in politics, law, administration, defence and
internal security. What has mainly caused these innovations
is that Africa, once freed from its colonial rulers, has had to
come to terms with its pre-colonial past. Peoples who stood
united against the alien in their midst have had to take desper-
ate measures to remain united in his absence. The myth of a
pre-colonial Golden Age to which Africa could return by
overthrowing its colonial masters has been shattered into
fragments. Africa now faces the stark fact that, for all its
achievements, its past was a divided past, which its colonial
rulers during their seventy-five years of power did comparatively little to overcome. It is therefore by studying its
pre-colonial past, rather than by imagining it, that Africa
will face its real problems. Fortunately, it shows every sign
of wishing to do so.

Index

98